P9-ECL-332

the
tucci
table

the tucci table

STANLEY TUCCI
and FELICITY BLUNT

with Kay Plunkett-Hogge

GALLERY BOOKS

NEW YORK   LONDON   TORONTO   SYDNEY   NEW DELHI

The author is donating 10 percent of his advance and 25 percent of any of his subsequent earnings from this book (in each case net of agency fees) to the Food Bank for New York City. To learn more, please visit foodbanknyc.org.

Gallery Books
A Division of Simon & Schuster, Inc.
1230 Avenue of the Americas
New York, NY 10020

Copyright © 2014 by Stanley Tucci

All rights reserved, including the right to reproduce this book or portions thereof in any form whatsoever. For information address Gallery Books Subsidiary Rights Department, 1230 Avenue of the Americas, New York, NY 10020

First Gallery Books hardcover edition October 2014

GALLERY BOOKS and colophon are registered trademarks of Simon & Schuster, Inc.

For information about special discounts for bulk purchases, please contact Simon & Schuster Special Sales at 1-866-506-1949 or business@simonandschuster.com.

The Simon & Schuster Speakers Bureau can bring authors to your live event. For more information or to book an event, contact the Simon & Schuster Speakers Bureau at 1-866-248-3049 or visit our website at www.simonspeakers.com.

Interior design by Jaime Putorti
Carol Roberts, indexer
Cover photography by Toby Lockebie

Manufactured in the United States of America

10 9 8 7 6 5 4 3 2 1

Library of Congress Cataloging-in-Publication Data
Tucci, Stanley.
 The Tucci table : cooking with family and friends / by Stanley Tucci and Felicity Blunt with Kay Plunkett-Hogge.
    pages cm
 Includes index.
 1. Cooking, Italian. 2. Cooking, British. 3. Tucci, Stanley—Friends and associates. I. Blunt, Felicity.
II. Plunkett-Hogge, Kay. III. Title.
 TX723T8324 2014
 641.5945—dc23
                2014018591

ISBN 978-1-4767-3856-7
ISBN 978-1-4767-3857-4 (ebook)

To my family, ever growing, ever hungry . . .

contents

Scones.

Mum's recipe

8oz S.K.
2oz Hard Marg.
Salt. 1 dessertspoon sugar.
1tsp. baking powder.
Milk to mix; soft. light.

Roll thickish.   Very hot oven.
Top tray.   15 minutes - 20.   Hot.

introduction

My life has been sustained by food beyond mere nourishment. The relationships forged by the acts of cooking and eating with others have had a profound effect on me and have more and more significance with every passing year. When I think of the moments that have brought me the most pleasure, the most joy, they are almost always framed within the context of food and the table. It is for this reason that this book exists.

A number of years ago, I helped put together a book for my culinary-loving parents and my friend Chef Gianni Scappin. Originally titled *Cucina e Famiglia* and later revised and reissued as *The Tucci Cookbook,* it was written to celebrate and safeguard the culinary history of our families—and this book does very much the same thing. I feel that so much of what shapes and binds a family is ephemeral. By this I mean that, besides photographs and home movies, families rely primarily on their oral histories of significant personal or familial events and experiences. Few families bother to write them down or even film a relative recounting them (although we all have reams of footage of the family pet doing something inane), and when it comes to recipes the same often holds true. We cook these familiar dishes the way we always have, without much thought because we know them well. But if they are never written down, tomorrow those recipes and the memories they fill us with will be gone forever.

My late wife, Kate, was a wonderful and generous cook. Our children—Isabel, Nicolo, and Camilla—and I have done our best to re-create many of her dishes because regretfully, save a couple, they were never written down. Making them now keeps her ever present in our lives, and, although they were delicious, what made them truly special was that they were *of her* and that she made them for us.

A few years ago, I was lucky enough to meet Felicity at her sister Emily's wedding. Whenever we chatted during that weekend the conversation inevitably turned to food; what dishes we loved, where we had eaten, and ultimately, by the end of the wedding, where we would eat together. When that fateful meal did transpire I bore witness to a passion and appetite for food and wine that rivaled my own (and perhaps those of Henry VIII and Bacchus combined). I have never seen so slender a person enjoy her food so much. I was rapt.

As we neared the end of our sybaritic repast and I was so stuffed I could barely breathe, I heard the woman who would one day be my wife innocently utter this query to a passing waiter: "Can we order a cheese plate?" I was agog. So was the waiter. She then turned her attention back to me and asked, "Where do you want to eat tomorrow?" I was in love.

In both the Tucci and the Blunt families, the act of eating together has always played a vital part. This book pays homage to our respective culinary traditions (mine from my grandparents and parents, Felicity's from her maternal grandmother), and expresses the new culinary traditions we are in the process of creating for the next generation. The following recipes are interpretations of dishes Felicity and I have enjoyed in restaurants, at friends' houses, or that we have created together over the last few years. They are an amalgam of our British and Italo-American palates, and they are dishes we think are worthy enough to put to paper and pass on to people and families who love to cook and eat as much as we do. With the guidance of our dear friend Kay Plunkett-Hogge and her extraordinary culinary knowledge, talent, literary skills, patience, humor, and fervent imagination, we have been able to write the book we'd wanted.

Both Felicity and I have a profound belief in the family meal, something that in our overscheduled lives is all but disappearing. The act of eating together, no matter how modest the meal, is an act of communion and celebration demonstrating that

we matter to one another. For us this also pertains to our wider family of friends and colleagues who have celebrated at the table with us over the years, some of whom have kindly shared their recipes and stories in this book.

The dinner table is the anvil upon which we forge our relationships. Be they ties of family, of friendship, of new love or of old, it is a place where we share the events of our day, our feelings, our stories, our memories, and our hopes and promises for the future.

Our family hopes that you and your family will find as much joy in these recipes as we do.

Stanley Tucci
London 2014

our essential equipment

The following things will make implementing the recipes in this book a little easier:

- ### TONGS
A very simple implement, but tongs are the one thing that I find indispensable.

- ### POTS AND PANS
I prefer good, heavy-bottomed copper or metal pots and pans. I also find a cast-iron skillet invaluable. In terms of sizes, simply put, small, medium, and large. An additional extra-large pot for making 2 pounds of pasta or stock and a 4- to 5-quart Dutch oven.

I don't care for nonstick pans. If I use a nonstick pan, I opt for a ceramic nonstick surface as opposed to Teflon. Green Pan and Bialetti make good ones.

- ### HEAT DIFFUSER
These stove top diffusers spread the heat evenly across the bottom of your pan and are essential for keeping a sauce on a really low simmer.

- MICROPLANE GRATER

You can use this for grating Parmigiano-Reggiano or nutmeg and for zesting citrus.

- MANDOLINE

Not a necessity, but very helpful for achieving consistently thin slices.

- METAL COLANDERS

Large enough to hold up to 2 pounds of pasta, and a couple of smaller ones for draining peas and other vegetables.

- SIEVES

One medium and one small sieve for sifting flour and draining rice, etc.

- METAL AND SILICONE SPATULAS, WOODEN SPOONS

One long metal spatula for turning fish to prevent it from breaking. A silicone spatula and wooden spoons for nonstick cookware (to avoid scratches) and for stirring risotto, as it's more gentle on the rice.

- KNIVES

A 5-inch chef's knife with a good weight, a paring knife, and a large 8-inch chopping knife. If you invest in three good quality knives, they should last for life. I prefer carbon steel or high-carbon steel—Suisin is a great brand.

- MORTAR AND PESTLE

Great for crushing garlic, herbs, etc.

- SMALL APPLIANCES

A food processor, an immersion blender, and a mini chopper will all come in handy for the recipes that follow.

OUR KITCHEN PANTRY ESSENTIALS

It goes without saying that we should all do our best to buy organic and local produce. However, this is not always possible for geographical, seasonal, or financial reasons. Unfortunately, buying organic can be quite expensive, but choosing the best quality ingredients available to you on your budget is essential to making the most of your meal.

THREE ESSENTIAL COOKING OILS

- Great extra virgin olive oil: Invest well and you will be repaid. Use this for dressings and seasonings. Much like wine, there is a variety of flavors and prices, so find what suits your palate best. I also like to keep a less expensive extra virgin olive oil on hand to add a little more flavor when needed.

- Regular olive oil: For sautéing.

- Vegetable oil: For deep-frying.

CANNED TUNA IN OLIVE OIL

- The best quality you can afford; I recommend Genoa or Pastene.

SAN MARZANO CANNED TOMATOES

- Best if they are whole, peeled—not crushed or pureed.

PASTA

- Brands we recommend: De Cecco, and if you are gluten intolerant as I am, Barilla and Le Veneziana—it tastes as close to the real thing as possible.

ONIONS, SHALLOTS, GARLIC, FRESH TOMATOES, AND LEMONS

- None of these ingredients needs to be kept in the fridge.

HERBS AND SPICES

- Coarse or kosher salt, black and green whole peppercorns, fresh rosemary, parsley, thyme, basil, bay leaves (dried or fresh), and good quality dried oregano.

WINE

- A good bottle of both red and white wine. (Don't cook with a wine you wouldn't drink.)

soups and salads

"During Felicity's first summer in New York, we planted a vegetable garden together. We made almost daily runs to the nursery to buy topsoil, compost, and manure to enrich the soil. Too much manure, it turned out, because everything tasted like sh*t. The only vegetables that flourished were the tomatoes. Having achieved the proper balance, our garden in London has successfully yielded zucchini, spring onions, runner beans, and, of course, tomatoes. We are still working on the lettuce."

—Stanley

tuscan tomato soup

This is a simple soup that I've been making for years. Right from the start, it was one of those things the kids loved to eat.

The secret to it lies in its slow simmer. When cooking anything with tomato, as my mother always says, you want it to lose its "tomato-y" taste. By this she means that you must slowly cook out the tomatoes' acidity or tinniness, allowing their sweetness to emerge.

Make sure you get the best canned tomatoes you can (see notes on San Marzano tomatoes, page xviii).

———————

1. For the soup, empty the tomatoes into a large bowl and crush them with your hands. Set aside.

2. In a large pot, heat 3 tablespoons of the olive oil over medium-high heat. Add the onion, shallot, if using, and garlic, and cook until they begin to soften—you do not want them to color. Stir in the tomatoes and two-thirds of the basil leaves and bring the mixture to a boil. Add the chicken stock and return to a boil. Season with salt and pepper, reduce the heat to low, and simmer, covered, for about 40 minutes.

3. For the croutons, in a sauté pan, heat 1 tablespoon of the olive oil over medium heat. Working in batches so as not to crowd the pan, fry the bread cubes until golden brown, setting them aside as you go. When they're all done, drizzle them with the remaining 1 teaspoon olive oil.

4. Serve the finished soup topped with the croutons and garnish with basil. Place the leftover croutons in a serving dish on the table for replenishing.

Serves 6 to 8

FOR THE SOUP

Two 28-ounce cans San Marzano plum tomatoes

3 tablespoons extra virgin olive oil

1 onion, finely chopped

1 small shallot, finely chopped (optional)

3 cloves garlic, finely chopped

10 to 12 fresh basil leaves, torn

16 ounces chicken stock, warm

Kosher salt and freshly ground black pepper

FOR THE CROUTONS

1 tablespoon plus 1 teaspoon extra virgin olive oil

4 cups dry Italian bread, cut into cubes

pea and ham hock soup

Serves 6

3 tablespoons olive oil

1 onion, finely chopped

2 cloves garlic, finely chopped

1 carrot, finely chopped

1 celery stalk, finely chopped

1 ham hock (1 to 1½ pounds)

6 cups chicken stock

2 quarts water

1 pound split peas

2 sprigs fresh thyme

1 bay leaf

Kosher salt and freshly ground black pepper

Extra virgin olive oil, for drizzling

Croutons (page 3), for garnish (optional)

When I first moved to New York, I couldn't afford to go out to restaurants. To be honest, I couldn't afford much. I would eat in coffee shops, because they were cheap, and most of them made great soup. This has always been one of my favorites.

Make sure you check the brand of split peas you buy. Some come presoaked so you can cook them straight out of the bag; others you'll need to soak in water for up to twenty-four hours before cooking.

———————

1. In a large heavy-bottomed saucepan, heat the olive oil over low to medium heat. Add the onion, garlic, carrot, and celery and cook until soft, 5 to 7 minutes.

2. Add the ham hock and toss to coat it with the oil and vegetables. Then add the stock, water, split peas, thyme, and bay leaf. Bring to a boil, then reduce the heat to low and simmer, partially covered, for about 1 hour.

3. Remove and discard the thyme and bay leaf. Remove the ham hock and set it aside.

4. With an immersion blender, blitz the soup in the pot until smooth. Season with salt and pepper. Shred the meat from the ham hock and add it to the soup.

5. Spoon into bowls and serve drizzled with a little extra virgin olive oil. Garnish with croutons, if you like.

STANLEY'S TIP

If the ham hock isn't entirely submerged in the liquid, turn it every now and then so that it cooks evenly and doesn't dry out.

emily's chicken noodle soup

My sister-in-law Emily is not only a great actress but a wonderful cook. This is one of her signature dishes.

Emily says: "I made this soup for my husband, John, and he says it may be the reason he wanted to *be* my husband. . . . Now, that's a lot to put on a soup, but hey, I'll take it. We always make it on a chilly night and slurp it down watching a movie. The ginger also kicks a cold in the teeth if you're feeling under the weather!"

—————

1. Preheat the oven to 400°F.

2. Finely dice one onion and set aside. Halve the remaining onion lengthwise, then cut it into chunky half-moon slices. Scatter the slices on a baking sheet. Place the chicken pieces on top. Tuck the thyme sprigs into the chicken, then brush it with a little of the olive oil and season with salt and pepper. Bake for 30 to 40 minutes. Remove from the oven and set aside to cool.

3. In a large cast-iron casserole, heat the remaining olive oil over medium heat. Add the diced onion, carrots, and celery, and sweat the vegetables, stirring occasionally, for about 5 minutes. Season them with a little salt and pepper.

4. Add the garlic and ginger, stir, and cook for 3 to 5 minutes more. Pour in the wine and let it cook down for a few minutes, then add the chicken broth and bouillon cubes and bring to a boil. Reduce the heat to maintain a very low simmer.

5. Remove the chicken skin and shred the meat roughly from the bones—the meat will become very tender and break down further in the soup. Add the shredded chicken to the soup, along with the onions and any juices from the baking sheet. These should be really

Serves 4 to 6

2 medium yellow onions

5 bone-in, skin-on chicken leg-and-thigh pieces

5 sprigs fresh thyme

2 tablespoons olive oil

Kosher salt and freshly ground black pepper

5 medium carrots, diced

4 celery stalks, diced

2 cloves garlic, finely diced

2½ tablespoons finely diced fresh ginger

½ cup dry white wine

8 cups low-sodium chicken broth

3 chicken bouillon cubes

2 tablespoons barbecue sauce (optional)

1 bay leaf

1 pound extra-wide egg noodles

recipe continued on next page

juicy and caramelized and will add great flavor. Stir in the barbecue sauce, if desired. (Emily says, "I don't know why I started doing this—it sounds a bit random, but I tried it once and I just think it adds a bit of a kick of flavor. I use the Bone Suckin' Sauce brand.")

6. Throw in a bay leaf and a couple of the chicken leg bones, cover, and cook at a very low simmer for about 2 hours.

7. When the soup is ready, remove from the heat, fish out the chicken bones and the bay leaf, and let it sit.

8. Meanwhile, bring a large pot of well-salted water to a boil. Add the egg noodles and cook according to the package directions. Drain and divide the noodles among serving bowls. Ladle the soup over the top to serve.

EMILY'S TIP

If you don't want to add noodles, the soup works really well without, too!

sunchoke soup
with crispy speck shards

Serves 4 to 6

3 slices speck or
prosciutto

Juice of 1 lemon

2 pounds sunchokes,
peeled

2 tablespoons butter

2 tablespoons olive oil

1 shallot, chopped

2 cloves garlic, chopped

Leaves from 2 sprigs
fresh thyme

4 cups chicken stock

Kosher salt and freshly
ground black pepper

Truffle oil, for drizzling

"Which way soever they be dressed and eaten, they stir and cause a filthy loathsome stinking wind within the body, thereby causing the belly to be pained and tormented, and are a meat more fit for swine than men!"
—John Goodyer, English botanist

Sunchokes, although known to cause a little gas, are nutty and delicious, with a flavor very close to mushrooms. For a family that doesn't consume a lot of lactose, they offer something creamy without the dairy. This soup is easy to prepare, tasty, and perfect for winter. Just be sure to eat this with people you love or, more important, who love you.

———————

1. Preheat the oven to 350°F.

2. Line a baking sheet with aluminum foil and lay the speck on top. Lay a second sheet of foil on top, and then set a second baking sheet on top to ensure that the speck stays flat as it cooks. Bake for 10 to 15 minutes. Remove and set aside until needed.

3. Fill a large bowl with water and add the lemon juice. Cut any larger sunchokes so that all the pieces are of a uniform size and place them immediately into the bowl of acidulated water so that they do not discolor.

4. Heat a large saucepan over low to medium heat and add the butter and olive oil. When the butter has melted, add the shallot and garlic and cook gently until soft but not colored. Add the thyme and stir. Drain the sunchokes and add them to the pan, stirring so that everything is evenly coated with the buttery mixture. Add the stock and bring to a boil, then reduce the heat to low and simmer gently until the sunchokes are soft—about 15 minutes or so. Season with salt and pepper.

5. Let the soup cool for a minute or so, then, using an immersion blender, blend until smooth. Take care not to splash yourself—the soup will still be extremely hot. Return to a gentle heat for a couple of minutes before pouring into serving bowls. Drizzle each portion with a little truffle oil and place a shard of the crisp speck on top.

potato and leek soup with fried parsley

This is a great idea for feeding the masses—kids, friends, drop-ins. It keeps fantastically well in the fridge and heats up quickly in portions for a quick lunch or supper. It's a hearty hot soup in the winter and refreshing when served cold in the summer. You can always throw in some kale or other leftover greens to add hardiness if you want to. The fried parsley topping is Felicity's, and a great addition.

———————

1. In a large saucepan or slow cooker, heat the oil and butter over medium-low heat. Add the onion, leeks, and garlic and cook gently, stirring often, until soft but not colored. This will take a good 15 to 20 minutes. Then add the stock and the potatoes, season with salt and pepper, and cook until the potatoes are soft, about 15 to 20 minutes.

2. While the potatoes are cooking, heat the vegetable oil in a small sauté pan until it is almost smoking. Fry the parsley sprigs in the hot oil for 30 seconds to 1 minute until they are crispy. Using a slotted spoon, remove the parsley and set aside on paper towels to drain excess oil.

3. When the potatoes are cooked, remove the soup from the heat, let cool slightly, and then blend with an immersion blender until smooth. Take care not to splash yourself—the soup will be very hot. Taste and adjust the seasoning. Reheat gently, if needed.

4. Serve in bowls, topping each with a sprig of fried parsley. Drizzle with the truffle oil, if using.

Serves 8 to 10

FOR THE SOUP

1 tablespoon olive oil

1 tablespoon butter

1 onion, finely chopped

3 leeks, chopped (about 1 pound)

2 cloves garlic, finely chopped

8 cups chicken stock

4 large potatoes (2 to 2¼ pounds), peeled and cubed

Kosher salt and freshly ground black pepper

Truffle oil, for drizzling (optional)

FOR THE FRIED PARSLEY

½ cup vegetable oil, for deep-frying

6 sprigs fresh flat-leaf parsley

STANLEY'S TIP

Leeks always seem to have a bit of mud in them. To clean, cut them in half lengthwise, starting halfway up the white portion and slicing all the way through the green ends. Fill a large jug with cold water and put in the leeks, green-end down. Swish them around, then drain. Repeat three or four times to be sure you've removed all the grit.

bistro green salad
with simple vinaigrette

Serves 4, as a side

**FOR THE
VINAIGRETTE**

½ shallot, minced

2 tablespoons white
wine vinegar

Good pinch of kosher
salt, plus more as
needed

1 teaspoon good quality
Dijon mustard (optional)

3 tablespoons olive oil

3 tablespoons vegetable
oil

FOR THE SALAD

1 to 2 heads butter
lettuce, thoroughly
washed and dried

This dressing complements the flavor of any green leaf. I find balsamic vinegar to be overused in dressings. A salad should cleanse the palate. In my family, we have salad at the end of the meal for this reason.

———————

1. In a bowl, mix together the shallot, vinegar, and salt, and let steep for a few minutes. Add the mustard (if using) to the vinegar mixture and stir well. Add the olive oil and vegetable oil. Blend the dressing with an immersion blender—it will turn into a thick, off-white emulsion—then taste. If it seems too sharp, add a bit more vegetable oil and a touch more salt, in increments, until the taste is balanced.

2. Dress the lettuce leaves with one-third to one-half of the dressing, mixing well, and serve at once. The leftover dressing will keep, covered, in the fridge for a few days.

cucumber and tomato salad

I love this light summer salad. The cucumbers are crisp and refreshing and the cherry tomatoes give the perfect pop of acidity.

With the tines of a fork, score the cucumbers to create some texture and then cut them crosswise into pennies. Put the salt in the bottom of a salad bowl and, using the garlic clove, rub it all over the bowl. Discard the garlic. Place the cucumber slices, tomato, and basil leaves in the bowl and gently dress the salad with a good glug of olive oil. Serve at once.

Serves 2 to 4

2 to 3 Kirby or Persian cucumbers

Good pinch of kosher salt

½ clove garlic

6 cherry tomatoes, halved

A few basil leaves, torn

Extra virgin olive oil

celery salad

Serves 4, as a side

1 teaspoon red wine vinegar

1 teaspoon rice vinegar

1 teaspoon white balsamic vinegar

Kosher salt and freshly ground black pepper

3 tablespoons extra virgin olive oil

4 stalks celery, chopped into ¼-inch pieces

We serve this dish—*insalata di sedano* in Italian—after a heavy risotto or hearty pasta dish, as it's bright and clean with a refreshingly sharp sweetness. The blend of vinegars lifts the dressing to another level, but if you don't have all three of them, just use 1 tablespoon of red wine vinegar instead.

———————

Whisk the vinegars together with salt and pepper to taste, then gently whisk in the oil until you have a smooth emulsion. Place the celery in an appropriate-sized bowl and toss with the dressing.

cucumber salad

Serves 2 to 4

2 to 3 Kirby or Persian cucumbers

Kosher salt

½ clove garlic

2 tablespoons extra virgin olive oil

1 tablespoon red wine vinegar

Freshly ground black pepper

Good pinch of dried oregano

This is another refreshing summer salad that my family has been making for generations.

———————

1. With the tines of a fork, score the cucumbers to create some texture and then cut them crosswise into pennies. Put a pinch of salt in the bottom of a salad bowl and, using the garlic clove, rub it all over the bowl. Discard the garlic. Place the cucumber slices in the bowl.

2. In a small bowl, whisk together the olive oil, vinegar, a pinch of salt, and pepper until you have an emulsified dressing. Pour enough of it over the cucumbers to coat lightly. Sprinkle with the oregano and serve at once.

quinoa salad with feta, pomegranate, and pistachio

Serves 4 as a main, 6 as a side

2 cups quinoa

3 tablespoons extra virgin olive oil

1½ tablespoons freshly squeezed lemon juice, or to taste

Kosher salt and freshly ground black pepper

6 tablespoons pomegranate seeds, plus 2 more tablespoons for serving

3 tablespoons salted pistachios or pine nuts, toasted

3 scallions, chopped

4 ounces feta cheese

1 blood orange, peeled and sliced into rounds (optional)

Extra virgin olive oil, for the orange (optional)

Felicity introduced me to this healthy alternative to pasta and bread—the staples of the Tucci family diet. Quinoa is a fantastic base to which so many other flavors can be added, like dates, avocado, or grilled halloumi cheese. Nutty, delicious, and good for you, this quinoa salad blends the sharpness of the feta, the sweetness of the pomegranate, and the crunch of the nuts. It can be served as a side or a main.

---

1. Soak the quinoa in cold water to remove its bitterness. Each brand is different, so check the instructions on the package. Then rinse it thoroughly.

2. Bring 3 to 4 cups salted water to a boil. Add the quinoa, reduce the heat to low, cover, and simmer for 15 to 20 minutes. The quinoa is done when the germ separates from the seed. It should have a little bite to it, too. Strain if necessary. Dress with the olive oil and lemon juice, season with salt and pepper, and set aside to cool.

3. Gently mix the pomegranate seeds, pistachios or pine nuts, and scallions into the quinoa. Taste and adjust the seasoning if necessary. Place the mixture in a serving dish and place the feta cheese on top. Scatter the last 2 tablespoons of pomegranate seeds over the top, gently break up the feta, and serve.

STANLEY'S TIP

This is delicious served with some sliced blood oranges dressed with extra virgin olive oil.

roasted potato salad

Serves 4 to 6

1 whole head garlic, top cut off to expose the cloves

Olive oil, for drizzling, plus 2 tablespoons

1 pound Yukon Gold potatoes

Kosher salt and freshly ground black pepper

¼ cup mayonnaise

½ tablespoon freshly squeezed lemon juice

½ to 1 teaspoon finely chopped fresh flat-leaf parsley (or dill, chervil, chives, tarragon— substitute any herb you like)

When you cook a lot, you hold so many recipes in your memory. My late wife, Kate, used to make a fantastic roasted potato salad. Unfortunately, she never wrote it down, but I have done my best to re-create it here.

———————

1. Preheat the oven to 450°F.

2. Drizzle the garlic head with a little olive oil and either wrap it in aluminum foil or put it in a terra-cotta garlic roaster.

3. Cut the potatoes, unpeeled, into 1½- to 2-inch chunks. Place them in a bowl with the olive oil and season with salt and pepper. Toss to coat. Spread the potatoes evenly on a baking sheet.

4. Place the garlic and the potatoes in the oven and roast them for 35 to 40 minutes, tossing and turning the potatoes about half-way through their cooking time. You want them golden and crisp. Remove and set aside on paper towels to cool completely. Remove the garlic and set aside to cool.

5. In a small bowl, thin the mayonnaise with the lemon juice, season with salt and pepper, and squeeze in 1 clove of the roasted garlic. In a large bowl, gently combine the mayonnaise dressing with the potatoes and add the chopped parsley. Peel the remaining roasted garlic and add it to the potatoes. Serve straight away for the best results—the longer you leave it, the more you'll lose the satisfying crunch on the potatoes.

cannellini bean and tuna salad with red onion

This is a simple, inexpensive salad that I often have for lunch, as I always have the majority of the ingredients on hand.

———————

Gently mix the tuna, beans, and onions together in a bowl. Season with salt and pepper, then toss with a glug of olive oil, followed by a good pinch of fresh parsley.

STANLEY'S TIP

For a little acidity, add a handful of halved cherry tomatoes at the end.

Serves 2 to 4

5-ounce can good tuna packed in olive oil, drained

15-ounce can cannellini beans, drained and rinsed

½ red onion, finely sliced into half-moons

Kosher salt and freshly ground black pepper

Extra virgin olive oil

Chopped fresh flat-leaf parsley

haricots verts with shallots and cherry tomatoes

The secret here is to just *barely* cook the haricots verts, as you want to preserve the crisp crunch of the green beans. You can do this well ahead of time as long as you soak them in ice water straight away. Always add the tomatoes at the last minute before serving to avoid them going soggy.

---

1. Bring a saucepan of salted water to a boil. Fill a large bowl with ice cubes and water and set aside. Blanch the haricots verts in the boiling water for 2 minutes, then transfer them immediately to the ice bath. Drain and dry them with paper towels.

2. Put the garlic and salt in a medium bowl and crush them together with a pestle or the back of a spoon. Add the mustard, shallot, vinegar, and pepper to taste, and whisk together. Gradually whisk in the olive oil until the mixture is emulsified.

3. Add the blanched haricots verts and the tomatoes and toss. Serve immediately.

Serves 4 to 6

8 ounces haricots verts, trimmed

½ clove garlic, finely chopped

1 teaspoon kosher salt

1 teaspoon Dijon mustard

1 small shallot, finely chopped

2 tablespoons white balsamic vinegar

Freshly ground black pepper

¼ cup extra virgin olive oil

3 ounces cherry tomatoes, halved

zucchini ribbon salad

Serves 4

3 zucchini

Juice of ½ lemon

Kosher salt and freshly
ground black pepper

¼ cup extra virgin olive
oil

A piece of Parmigiano-
Reggiano or pecorino,
for shaving

Felicity made this for dinner one night without really thinking about it, and I loved it. It's light, easy to prepare, and the texture is really lovely. If you find that you've forgotten to make a salad, it's the perfect remedy, as it's incredibly simple and quick.

———————

1. Roughly peel the zucchini and discard the darker skin, which can be very bitter. With a potato peeler, shave each zucchini into ribbons, discarding the soggy interior seeds. Set the zucchini ribbons aside in a bowl.

2. In a small bowl, season the lemon juice with salt and pepper and whisk together. Add the olive oil and whisk again until you have a smooth emulsion. Taste the dressing and adjust the seasoning to your liking.

3. Toss the zucchini with the dressing and, using your potato peeler, shave the Parmigiano over the top to taste. Serve at once; otherwise, the ribbons will lose their texture.

FELICITY'S TIP

You can make the same salad with shaved carrot ribbons, in which case, leave out the Parmigiano.

ryan's kale and amino acid salad

Serves 4 to 6

1 pound baby kale or black kale

1 large sweet or Vidalia onion, diced

¼ cup extra virgin olive oil

¼ cup grape seed oil

2 tablespoons plus 1 teaspoon Bragg Liquid Aminos

1 teaspoon kosher salt

Juice of 1 large lemon

1 teaspoon apple cider vinegar

¼ teaspoon red pepper flakes

¼ cup Bragg nutritional yeast flakes, plus more for serving

We had this delicious salad at the house of a friend of ours who is lucky enough to have an extraordinary chef named Ryan Toal. Ryan had made a feast of fish, meat, and fowl, but this salad was a revelation. The dressing—amino acids, lemon juice, vinegar, and nutritional yeast flakes—tenderizes the leaves and breaks down into a creamy coating.

Ryan says: "Baby kale is not always available at the farmers' market. So I often use black kale, which you can get at your local Whole Foods Market any day of the week—I like it just as much, if not more, for this recipe. I sometimes make the same salad with an Asian spin on it, by leaving out the yeast, replacing the liquid aminos with soy sauce, adding in sesame oil and some sesame seeds, and using less extra virgin olive oil."

———————

1. If using black kale, strip the leaves off their stalks, then wash and dry them. Roughly chop or slice the black kale into wide ribbons. Baby kale can be left whole. Place the kale in a large bowl and add the onion, olive oil, grape seed oil, liquid aminos, salt, lemon juice, and vinegar. Toss it all together and set the mixture aside for 30 minutes, tossing it periodically. This can be done up to 2 hours before serving, but if you'll be holding the salad for more than 30 minutes, store it in the refrigerator or it will become soggy.

2. Just before serving, add the red pepper flakes and nutritional yeast to the salad and toss gently. Once the nutritional yeast has been added, the dressing should take on an almost creamy consistency.

3. Serve this salad in a large chilled bowl topped with an extra shake of nutritional yeast.

puntarella salad
with anchovy dressing

Every time I go to Riva, one of our local Italian restaurants here in London, I order this salad. Called *puntarelle con acciuge* in Italian, this recipe features the crisp, sharp flavor of chicory, with its undertones of fennel and a crunch reminiscent of celery, and anchovies. This is my own version of this classic Roman dish.

————

1. To make the salad: First, prepare the puntarella: Trim off any ragged outer leaves and discard. Separate the leafy green fronds from the paler spines. Cut the spines lengthwise into thin strips, and then cut the strips into manageable lengths, 4 to 5 inches, and slice the inner spears into similar size strips. Soak the puntarella in ice water for at least 1 hour to remove some of its bitterness.

2. To make the dressing: Chop the anchovies into small pieces and place them in a mortar. Using a pestle, mash them together with the garlic. Season with pepper and stir in the lemon juice. Add the olive oil and stir until emulsified.

3. Drain and dry the puntarella thoroughly, then place it in a large bowl and dress it. You shouldn't need any salt, thanks to the anchovies, but taste it and add some if necessary. Serve immediately.

Serves 4

FOR THE SALAD

1 head puntarella

FOR THE DRESSING

4 to 8 canned anchovy fillets, rinsed

1 clove garlic

Freshly ground black pepper

2 tablespoons freshly squeezed lemon juice

¼ cup extra virgin olive oil

Kosher salt (optional)

cicchetti

small plates

"*Cicchetti* are both a way of making guests feel welcome, and a way to stave off ever-hungry children who never stop asking, 'when will dinner be ready?'"

—Felicity

frittata

Serves 2

5 to 6 large eggs

3 to 4 tablespoons olive oil

Kosher salt

Good pinch of chopped fresh flat-leaf parsley (optional)

Good pinch of freshly grated Parmigiano-Reggiano

Freshly ground black pepper

The movie *Big Night* ends with my character, Secondo, cooking a frittata. As it was always my intention to shoot that scene in a master shot with no coverage (in a single continuous shot, making it impossible to edit), it was crucial that I learned to make the frittata properly. Luckily for me, Chef Gianni Scappin was a great teacher. It is necessary that you have the right pan, by which I mean one that you feel comfortable with, and the best eggs you can lay your hands on.

The great thing about this dish is that you can add whatever you like to it: sautéed potatoes, sautéed mushrooms, grilled scallions, leftover peas, et cetera. Just stir them into the egg mixture and you will have a rich but simple meal.

———————

1. Crack the eggs into a bowl and beat them gently with a fork for a minute or so, making sure you angle the bowl so that you really blend them well. You could use a whisk instead of a fork, if you prefer, but you will end up with a puffier-textured frittata.

2. In a 10-inch sauté pan with sloping sides, heat the olive oil over medium-high heat. You want to get it pretty hot, and tilt the pan to make sure the sides of the pan are well coated. When the oil is hot, season the eggs with salt and add the parsley (if using), then pour the mixture into the pan. Scramble the eggs vigorously with a silicone spatula, tipping and moving the pan continuously and drawing the egg from the sides into the middle. Keep the pan moving to make sure the egg doesn't stick. Add the Parmigiano and a good grinding of pepper. Then flip or turn the frittata and cook for a minute or so more, until golden and cooked through. Serve immediately.

sausage rolls

Makes 12 to 16 rolls

2 tablespoons olive oil

2 shallots, diced

1 clove garlic, diced

14 ounces sausage meat (about 6 sausages, preferably Cumberland)

Leaves from 3 sprigs fresh thyme, chopped

Leaves from 1 sprig fresh rosemary, finely chopped

Pinch of kosher salt

Pinch of freshly ground black pepper

1 package puff pastry, chilled; if frozen, defrosted and kept chilled

Flour, for dusting

1 large egg, beaten

This is an English classic from Felicity's childhood. The combination of herby, juicy meat and crisp, buttery puff pastry is irresistable. It's really easy to make and it's great to have out for the kids when they come back from school. You just need some well-sourced sausage meat (see Stanely's Tip next page) and some store-bought pastry.

I like to add rosemary and thyme—they are two of my favorite herbs—but sage also works beautifully with sausage meat. The most important thing is to get good quality sausage. The cheaper stuff tends to be packed with water, which it releases as it cooks, giving your rolls soggy bottoms!

---

1. Preheat the oven to 350°F.

2. In a sauté pan, heat the olive oil over low heat. Add the shallot and garlic and cook until they are translucent and soft. Set aside.

3. Remove the sausage meat from the casings and place it in a bowl, discarding the casings. Add the thyme, rosemary, salt, and pepper, as well as the shallot and garlic. Mix together well with your hands.

4. Remove the puff pastry from the fridge and place it on a floured surface. Cut it in half. Place half of the sausage mixture in a long row down the center of each half. Brush the edges of the pastry with the beaten egg and then fold the pastry over the sausage and seal the edges. Seal the ends carefully as well. Take a knife and make slashes halfway through the roll all the way down its length (you should end up with about eight segments). This will help the sausage meat cook all the way through the roll. Brush the pastry all over with egg and bake for 25 to 30 minutes, until the sausage is cooked and the pastry is fully puffed and golden.

5. Remove from the oven and cut the rolls all the way through the slashes, forming segments. Let cool a little before serving.

STANLEY'S TIP

Myers of Keswick in New York City stocks fantastic British sausage meat and will deliver nationwide.

recipe pictured on next page

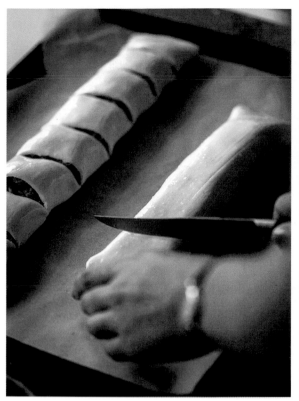

risotto cakes

Makes 20 to 24 cakes

2 cups room-temperature risotto (see Basic Risotto, page 67)

2 eggs, lightly beaten

¼ cup freshly grated Parmigiano-Reggiano

Kosher salt

2 cups fine bread crumbs

3 tablespoons olive oil

3 tablespoons vegetable oil

Freshly ground black pepper

As with pasta, when I make risotto I try to make more than I need, so I'll have some left over. These risotto cakes are a great side dish, and they're a perfect snack in their own right. When I was shooting *The Devil Wears Prada*, I brought some for lunch and gave one to my new friend Emily Blunt, who inhaled it in keeping with what I was soon to learn is the eating practice of all of the Blunts.

————

1. In a bowl, combine the risotto, eggs, cheese, and salt. Cover and refrigerate for about 20 minutes to firm up until ready to roll.

2. Place the bread crumbs in a shallow dish. Form the cold risotto mixture into 2½-inch balls. Passing them back and forth between your hands, flatten the balls into patties and coat them in the bread crumbs, letting any excess bread crumbs fall away. Place them on some waxed or parchment paper on a tray or platter, and put them back in the fridge for up to 30 minutes.

3. In a 12-inch sauté pan, heat 1½ tablespoons of the olive oil and 1½ tablespoons of the vegetable oil over low heat. When the oil is hot, gently place a few of the risotto cakes into the pan and cook for 3 to 5 minutes until golden brown. Flip the risotto cakes and cook for 3 to 5 minutes more, until the second side is golden brown. Make sure you gently lift them to check that the underside is golden and crisp before turning to brown the other side.

4. When they are done to your liking, use a spatula to transfer the risotto cakes to paper towels to drain. Carefully wipe out the pan with excess paper towels to remove any stray bread crumbs. Heat the remaining 1½ tablespoons olive oil and 1½ tablespoons vegetable oil and continue as above until you have cooked all of the risotto cakes.

5. Season with salt and pepper. Serve hot or cold.

STANLEY'S TIP

When served with a green salad, these make a great lunch, and alongside fried eggs, a fantastic breakfast.

tony shalhoub's stuffed grape leaves

I've been lucky enough to have worked with and been friends with the incredibly talented Tony Shalhoub for the past twenty-five years. Although we only pretended to be brothers in *Big Night,* I still pretend he is my brother in real life. I first had these stuffed grape leaves when I visited Tony and he was preparing them for an extended family feast. I thought they were extraordinary then, and still do now.

Tony says: "We always use fresh grape leaves when they are in season and available. But whether you're using fresh or jarred leaves, always remove the stem at the base of the leaf. I always prefer to use just ground lamb. Some prefer ground beef, and a lot of people prefer a combination—dealer's choice."

————————————

1. In a bowl, mix together the ground meat, onion, tomatoes, cinnamon, garam masala (if using), and salt and pepper to taste. Take 1 teaspoon of the mixture and fry it in a little olive oil, just to check the seasoning. Adjust as necessary. Mix in the rice, cover, and set aside.

2. Line the bottom of a large pot with the lemon slices and set aside.

3. In a separate large pot, bring 2 quarts of water to a boil over high heat. Drop in the grape leaves and turn off the heat. If you are using fresh grape leaves, let them soak for 1 minute, then drain and refresh the leaves in ice water. If you are using jarred leaves, let them soak for a good 20 minutes, then drain them well on paper towels. Trim the stem at the base of each leaf.

4. Separate the leaves and lay them flat on your work surface. Spoon some of the meat mixture onto the veiny side of each leaf. You want just enough of the filling to make each leaf plump, but

Makes 50 to 60 stuffed grape leaves, serves a lot

1 pound ground lamb

1 large onion, chopped

2 whole tomatoes, blanched and peeled

2 tablespoons ground cinnamon, plus more for dusting

1 tablespoon garam masala (optional)

Kosher salt and freshly ground black pepper

1 cup long-grain white rice, rinsed

1 lemon, thinly sliced

50 to 60 fresh grape leaves or 1 large jar grape leaves

½ cup freshly squeezed lemon juice

Plain Greek yogurt, for dipping

recipe continued on next page

not so much that it can't be closed and contained. (Tony says that he finds 1 table-spoon of the filling is about enough for a medium grape leaf, but the amount will vary depending on the size of each leaf.) Fold in the ends of the leaves and roll them closed from one side. Make sure you don't pack them too tightly—the rice will expand as it cooks and you don't want them to burst.

5. Arrange the rolled leaves, seam-side down, side-by-side on the lemon slices and then on top of each other in layers. (Tony says it's best to start at the outside of the pan and work your way in.) Add just enough water to cover the rolls, then add the lemon juice and an extra sprinkling of cinnamon. Set a small plate or a lid smaller than the circumference of your pan on top of the rolls to hold them down. Bring the liquid to a boil over high heat and cook for 3 minutes. Reduce the heat to low, cover the pot tightly, and simmer for about 1 hour, or until the rice is cooked.

6. Serve at room temperature with some plain Greek yogurt alongside for dipping.

fried calamari

Calamari, if cooked properly, should not be soggy and oily but instead pearly, tender rings of flesh coated in a light and crispy batter. Kids who would never touch squid love these; a plate is gone in thirty seconds.

———————

1. Clean the squid thoroughly. Cut the bodies into slices about ¼-inch thick and trim the longer pieces of the tentacles. Put them in a bowl, add enough milk to cover them, and refrigerate for a couple of hours. This will soften the flesh.

2. Fill a deep-fryer with oil and heat to 350°F. Alternatively, heat 2 to 3 inches of oil in a large, heavy-bottomed pan over medium-high heat until it registers 350°F on a deep-fry thermometer. If you are using the pan method, be very careful and ensure you take all appropriate precautions.

3. Place the flour in a shallow dish and season it with the oregano and plenty of salt and pepper. Remove the squid from the milk and dredge it in the seasoned flour—the milk will help the flour stick to the flesh. Working in batches, fry the squid in the hot oil until golden brown—1 to 2 minutes. Using a slotted spoon, transfer the fried squid to paper towels to drain the excess oil. Repeat the process until all the squid is cooked.

4. Serve with lemon wedges and some of Felicity's Cheat's Aioli (page 219).

FELICITY'S TIP

If you can't find any fresh squid, frozen will do. Just make sure it is fully defrosted.

Serves 4 to 6

6 medium or 8 small squid

Whole milk

Vegetable oil, for deep-frying

1½ cups all-purpose flour

1 teaspoon dried oregano

Kosher salt and freshly ground black pepper

Lemon wedges, for serving

Felicity's Cheat's Aioli (page 219), for serving

grilled cheese with pesto and prosciutto

Makes 1 sandwich

1 tablespoon pesto sauce

2 slices good Italian bread

2 to 4 slices good melting cheese, such as mozzarella, soft pecorino, or goat cheese

2 to 3 slices prosciutto

2 tablespoons olive oil

This is, literally, just a grilled cheese sandwich with pesto and prosciutto in it. It makes a perfect snack.

———

1. Spread the pesto sauce on one side of each slice of bread. Layer the cheese and prosciutto over the pesto and close the sandwich, pressing down firmly.

2. In a heavy cast-iron pan, heat the olive oil. When it is nice and hot, place the sandwich in the pan and, if you have one, weigh it down with a bacon press. If you don't have a bacon press, use a metal spatula to press down on the sandwich so that you get a good, compact grilled sandwich. Cook the sandwich for 2 to 3 minutes, then flip it carefully and do the same on the other side until you have crisp, golden bread and oozing cheese.

STANLEY'S TIP

Manchego cheese is also delicious, although it's not as "melty" as the others.

pissaladière

My friend Natasha Richardson, who passed away far too young, was an extraordinary cook who threw some of the best dinner parties I have ever attended. Her sister and mother were kind enough to cobble together the notes that Natasha had made about this recipe, which was one of my favorites. I have it with a glass, or three, of rosé (which Natasha called "French water"), and remember my dear friend and the many great meals we had together. She is sorely missed.

The base can be made of our pizza dough base or a sheet of puff pastry, depending on your preference. If you're using the dough, you will only need half of it. I suggest freezing the other half or using it to make the rustic pizza described in the Tip following this recipe.

Serves 4

¼ cup olive oil

2 tablespoons butter

2½ to 3 pounds onions, finely sliced

4 cloves garlic, coarsely chopped

Leaves from 4 sprigs fresh thyme

1 teaspoon soft light brown sugar

Kosher salt and freshly ground black pepper

1 sheet puff pastry or 1 portion Pizza Dough (page 214)

Flour for dusting if using pizza dough

16 anchovy fillets

Handful of black olives

---

1. In a large frying pan, heat the olive oil and butter over medium heat. Add the onions and soften them for 5 to 10 minutes, then add the garlic, thyme, and brown sugar. If your frying pan is overcrowded, start by using two frying pans and transfer the onions to one once they have shrunk in size. Reduce the heat and continue to cook gently until the onions start to caramelize and are meltingly tender (this may be a good time to use a heat diffuser). This could take up to an hour or more. Season with salt and pepper to taste. Remove from the heat and set aside.

2. Preheat the oven to 425°F. Line a baking sheet with parchment paper.

3. If using puff pastry: Unroll the puff pastry and give it a quick roll with a rolling pin. Place it on the prepared baking sheet. Then score a line about 1 inch from the edges on each side of the pastry—this

recipe continued on next page

will give your tart a raised edge. Pile the onions onto the pastry, keeping them inside the scored lines. Place the anchovies on top in a diamond pattern, and place an olive in the middle of each diamond.

4. Bake for about 20 minutes, or until the pastry edges are puffed and golden and the onions are hot throughout and beginning to brown.

5. If using pizza dough: Make a portion of the pizza dough on page 214, following the method up to the point where the dough has risen for the first time.

6. When it has proofed, divide the dough into two portions. Lightly oil a 10-by-14-inch baking sheet and sprinkle it with a little flour. Spread out a portion of the dough on the tray, pushing it to the edges of the pan. Cover the dough with plastic wrap and set aside in a warm place for 30 to 40 minutes. You can freeze the second portion of your dough for later use.

7. When it has proofed again, remove the plastic wrap and spread the onions over the top, and finish as above with the anchovies and olives. Bake for about 15 minutes, or until the dough is cooked golden brown and the onions are hot.

8. Serve hot, room temperature, or cold.

STANLEY'S TIP

If you are using pizza dough and want to make a rustic pizza with the remaining dough, follow the method above, but instead of putting onions, olives, and anchovies on top, just drizzle the dough with some good olive oil, your choice of fresh rosemary or thyme, and a sprinkling of kosher salt. Bake for 10 to 12 minutes until golden and crisp. Cut into squares. This is perfect with wine, cheese, and olives.

pasta, rice, and grains

"One summer, Stanley took me to Martha's Vineyard and introduced me to the joys of clamming. We went kayaking with the whole family in a well-loved cove, and then the real business of clamming began. I was so excited. But every time I thought I'd found a prize clam, it turned out to be a crab, which would firmly grab my thumb with its pincers. Everyone else filled bucket after bucket with the good stuff, which made for a delicious *spaghetti vongole*, which I devoured whilst tending to my wounds."

—Felicity

spaghetti vongole

There used to be a restaurant at the Museum of Modern Art in New York called Sette Moma that overlooked the peaceful oasis of the sculpture garden. I would often go there to write, as they were kind enough to let me stay at a table for long periods of time and order very little. Without fail, I would have this dish. I loved the way they prepared it: with a touch of fresh tomato and peperoncini. The restaurant is gone now but the owner, Gianfranco Sorrentino, still has two wonderful restaurants in New York, Il Gattopardo on East 54th Street and The Leopard on West 67th, where this dish is still served.

Look for the small *vongole* (clams) at the fish market, as they are the sweetest. In England, they are known as Palourde or Poole clams.

---

1. First, clean the clams, discarding any with broken shells or that won't close when you tap them. Place them in a large bowl of cold water with the cornmeal for about half an hour. Then drain and rinse to wash away any grit or sand.

2. Bring a large pot of salted water to a boil. Cook the spaghetti according to the instructions on the package.

3. Meanwhile, in a heavy-bottomed sauté pan, heat the olive oil over low heat. Add the garlic and the peperoncini, and cook until the garlic is fragrant but not colored. Raise the heat to medium and add the clams, shaking the pan and stirring to coat them in the oil and garlic.

4. Add a good amount of salt and ground pepper. Add the parsley and toss to coat the clams once more. Put the lid on. Cover the pan and cook, shaking the pan every so often until the clams are open and cooked, about 3 minutes. Discard any that do not open.

5. When the pasta and the clams are done, drain the spaghetti, and put it in the pan with the clams, and toss it through. Garnish with a little extra chopped fresh parsley and serve at once.

Serves 4

2 pounds fresh vongole (clams)

1 tablespoon cornmeal

1 pound spaghetti

¼ cup extra virgin olive oil

3 cloves garlic, cut into slivers

2 to 4 small dried Italian peperoncini

Kosher salt and freshly ground black pepper

1 large handful fresh flat-leaf parsley, chopped, plus more for serving

pasta with fresh cherry tomatoes and basil

Serves 4 to 6

1 pound pasta (capellini, linguine, or spaghetti)

3 tablespoons extra virgin olive oil

1 small onion, finely chopped

1 clove garlic, minced

1 pound ripe cherry tomatoes, halved

1 tablespoon salt

1 cup fresh basil leaves, torn, plus more for serving

Freshly grated Parmigiano-Reggiano, for serving

Pasta alla checca, as this dish is called in Italy, is quick, light and fresh, and perfect for the summer months when tomatoes are in abundance and at their peak. When I was working a lot in Los Angeles, it seemed that every restaurant had it on their menu—which is hardly surprising: they have access to terrific tomatoes year-round.

————

1. Bring a large pot of salted water to a boil. Cook the pasta according to the directions on the package until al dente.

2. Meanwhile, in a 12-inch sauté pan, heat the olive oil over low heat. Add the onion and garlic and cook over gentle heat (use a diffuser for this—see Our Essential Equipment, page xv), stirring occasionally, until softened but not colored. Then add the tomatoes and raise the heat to high. Add the salt, and toss everything together. Cook for a couple of minutes *only*, then throw in the torn basil to wilt it. The tomatoes' juices will emulsify with the oil, creating a sauce.

3. When the pasta and the sauce are done, remove the spaghetti from the water with tongs and add it directly to the sauce, tossing them together—you may need to divide both the sauce and the pasta and do this in two batches. Taste and adjust the seasoning, if necessary. Transfer to serving bowls and sprinkle with extra fresh basil, if you like. Serve with some freshly grated Parmigiano on the side.

nico's pasta with prosciutto, onions, peas, and pancetta

Serves 4 to 6

1 pound fettuccini

2 tablespoons olive oil

1 whole onion, finely chopped

1 small shallot, finely chopped

½ clove garlic, sliced

2 cups pancetta, coarsely diced

4 slices prosciutto

¼ cup chicken stock

1 cup frozen peas, thawed

3 tablespoons freshly grated Parmigiano-Reggiano

Chopped fresh flat-leaf parsley

Kosher salt and freshly ground black pepper

2 eggs (optional)

2 egg yolks (optional)

This is my son Nico's favorite pasta: he loves prosciutto and onions. Like all kids, his tastes are constantly changing and developing. Just a little while ago he wouldn't even touch an onion. However, if you like eggs, as I do, then add them to create a luscious carbonara.

———————

1. Bring 8 quarts salted water to a rolling boil. Cook the fettuccini according to the directions on the package until al dente.

2. Meanwhile, in a large sauté pan, heat the olive oil over medium heat. Add the onion, shallot, and garlic. Cook until tender, about 5 minutes. Remove from the pan and set aside. Add the pancetta to the sauté pan and cook over medium-high heat until the fat has mostly rendered and the pancetta is crispy and golden. Add the prosciutto about halfway through this process, as it will take less time to cook than the pancetta. Return the onion-shallot-garlic mixture to the pan with a couple of tablespoons of the stock, mix it all together, and continue cooking for 2 minutes more. Add the peas and the remaining stock and cook for 2 minutes more.

3. Drain the pasta, reserving ½ cup of the pasta cooking water. Toss the pasta with the sauce in the pan on medium heat. Remove the pan from the heat and, if not using the carbonara finish, toss with the Parmigiano, parsley, and salt and pepper to taste. Add some or all of the reserved pasta cooking water if the final mixture of sauce and pasta seems too dry. Transfer to a platter and serve immediately.

FOR THE CARBONARA FINISH: In a bowl, whisk the eggs and the egg yolks together with 1 tablespoon of the Parmigiano and some pepper. Remove the pasta from the heat (very important) and add the eggs, stirring them through the pasta until they form a creamy coating on the pasta. The hot pasta will cook the eggs through. Add the remaining 2 tablespoons Parmigiano and the parsley and toss. Again, if the final mixture of sauce and pasta seems dry, add some or all of the reserved pasta cooking water and toss. Transfer to a platter and serve immediately.

pasta with mushrooms

Serves 4 to 6

½ cup dried porcini mushrooms soaked in 1 cup of warm water

4 tablespoons olive oil

2 tablespoons butter

1 large onion, finely chopped

2 cloves garlic, finely chopped

1 shallot, finely chopped

Kosher salt

2½ to 3 pounds brown mushrooms (such as chestnut or baby Portobello), trimmed and thinly sliced

1 bouquet garni (1 sprig rosemary, 1 leaf of sage, 1 sprig thyme)

¾ cup dry white wine

1 cup chicken or veal stock

Freshly ground black pepper

1½ cups grated Parmigiano-Reggiano

1 pound dried pappardelle

1 tablespoon chopped fresh flat-leaf parsley, for serving

Mushrooms can be used in myriad ways: as a side, served with polenta, and of course with pasta. This mushroom *ragù*, or *pasta con funghi* as it is known in Italy, is a favorite of both Nico's and my dad's. You can change the notes of the sauce just by using veal stock as opposed to chicken stock.

————————

1. First, soak the dried porcini in 1 cup of warm water for about 30 minutes. Then lift them from the soaking water and squeeze out as much of the water as you can, saving all the liquid. Pour the soaking liquid through a coffee filter into a bowl to remove any sediment. Finely chop the porcini and set aside.

2. In a large sauté pan, heat 3 tablespoons of the olive oil and a tablespoon of butter over low heat. Add the onion, garlic, and shallots and cook until softened but not brown. Raise the heat to medium. Add another tablespoon of olive oil, a teaspoon of salt, all of the brown mushrooms, the chopped dried mushrooms, and the bouquet garni. Cover and sauté until the mushrooms have softened a bit, about 5 minutes. Add the white wine and let it cook down uncovered for about 1 minute. Add the reserved dried porcini soaking liquid, the chicken stock, and a good pinch of black pepper. Lower the heat to medium-low and cook until the mushrooms are nice and soft, 20 to 25 minutes. Remove the bouquet garni and gently stir in the remaining tablespoon of butter. Add salt and pepper to taste.

3. Bring 6 quarts of well-salted water to a boil. Cook the pappardelle according to the directions on the package until al dente.

4. Drain the pasta and toss it in the pan with the mushrooms. (You may have to divide the sauce and the pasta into two batches to do this.) Turn off the heat, add one cup of the Parmigiano, and toss it through the pasta. To serve, transfer the pasta to a platter and top with the remaining Parmigiano and the parsley.

STANLEY'S TIP

A heat diffuser can be used to keep your heat consistent, allowing you to cook long and slow.

bolognese

Serves 6 to 8

2 celery stalks

2 carrots

2 cloves garlic

2 onions

3 tablespoons olive oil

3 tablespoons butter

1 ounce pancetta, very finely chopped or minced

2 pounds ground beef

Kosher salt and freshly ground black pepper

1⅓ cups red wine

2 bay leaves

Leaves from 2 sprigs fresh thyme

One 14-ounce can whole San Marzano tomatoes, crushed by hand

1 cup whole milk (lactose-free is fine)

1 pound pasta (fettuccine or pappardelle works best)

Freshly grated Parmigiano-Reggiano, for serving

You would be hard-pressed to find a child—or an adult—who doesn't like Bolognese sauce. Make a big batch so you can freeze some to always have on hand.

Cook this long and slow to extract every last ounce of flavor. It becomes even more flavorful if cooked a day in advance.

———————

1. Finely chop the celery, carrot, garlic, and onion. You can also pulse them in a blender, but be sure they retain some integrity and don't turn into a paste. (I often do the onion and garlic together, then the carrot and celery together, and then I combine them all in a bowl.) Set aside.

2. In a large heavy-bottomed saucepan, heat the oil and butter over low to medium heat. Be careful not to let the butter burn. Add the pancetta, just to soften it. Then add the celery, carrot, garlic, and onion mixture and stir to coat well. Sweat the vegetables in the pan, stirring every now and then, for a good 10 to 12 minutes. You want them to melt and break down. Then add the meat, crumbling it in with your hands as you go. Leave it to sear and take on color. Turn it often with a spoon or spatula to make sure the meat is browned and has "caught" the bottom of the pan a little.

3. Season with the salt and pepper. Add the wine and bring to a simmer to cook out the alcohol. Add the bay leaves, thyme, and tomatoes, and stir to combine. Bring the sauce to a boil, then reduce the heat to maintain a gentle simmer and cook until it has reduced slightly, 5 to 10 minutes. Add the milk. Cover the pan, reduce the heat to low, and simmer very gently for 1 to 1½ hours. Taste and adjust the seasoning.

4. Meanwhile, bring a large pot of salted water to a boil. Cook the pasta according to the directions on the package. Drain the pasta.

5. Serve the sauce over the pasta, topped with a good grating of Parmigiano.

STANLEY'S TIP

A heat diffuser can be used to keep your heat consistent, allowing you to cook long and slow.

orecchiette with broccoli rabe and anchovies

Our friend and cookery writer, Kay, picked up this recipe on her honeymoon in Puglia. It's very typical of the region—vegetable-led with the *cime di rape* (in Italian) or rapini and finished with a salty accent of anchovy. I love it, though I probably prefer it a little less spicy than she does.

------

1. Bring a large pot of salted water to a boil. Blanch the broccoli rabe in the boiling water until just soft, 1 to 2 minutes. Scoop out the broccoli rabe with a slotted spoon, leaving the water in the pot, and refresh it under cold running water to stop the cooking. Once it has cooled a little, chop it into rough chunks and set aside.

2. Bring the pot of water back to a boil. Add the orecchiette and cook according to the directions on the package until just al dente.

3. Meanwhile, in a sauté pan, heat the olive oil over medium heat. Add the garlic cloves and cook to infuse the oil with their flavor. Do not allow them to color. Remove the garlic from the pan and discard it. Add the anchovies and peperoncini and cook gently until the anchovy has dissolved into the oil. Then add the chopped broccoli rabe and cook everything together until heated through and well combined.

4. Drain the orecchiette, reserving a bit of the pasta cooking water. Add the pasta to the pan with the sauce. Add a little of the reserved pasta cooking water if it seems a little dry. Season to taste and serve.

Serves 6

1 pound broccoli rabe, trimmed

1 pound orecchiette

3 to 4 tablespoons olive oil

4 cloves garlic

8 anchovies, drained and chopped

1 to 2 whole dried peperoncini, crumbled

Kosher salt and freshly ground black pepper

uova da raviolo

ravioli filled with egg yolk

Makes 6 large ravioli, serves 6 as a starter

FOR THE FILLING

½ cup ricotta

½ cup finely grated Parmigiano-Reggiano

3 cups loosely packed baby spinach, blanched, squeezed dry, and finely chopped

Zest of ½ lemon

Good grating of fresh nutmeg

Leaves from 1 sprig of fresh thyme

Kosher salt and freshly ground black pepper

TO ASSEMBLE

1 portion Pasta Dough (page 211)

6 good, fresh egg yolks

4 to 6 tablespoons butter

Freshly grated Parmigiano-Reggiano, for serving

Felicity and I first tried this extraordinarily decadent dish on our honeymoon in Piemonte: a single pillow of feathery pasta filled with ricotta and a whole egg yolk, which, when cut open, releases all the richness inside. We were a little nervous the first time we made it at home, but it turned out to be easier than we thought, and a lot of fun. Make sure you use the best eggs you can find, as they will make all the difference.

———

1. Make the filling: In a large bowl, stir together the ricotta, Parmigiano, spinach, lemon zest, nutmeg, and thyme and season well with salt and pepper. Set aside.

2. Assemble the ravioli: Roll out the pasta dough as directed on page 211. Cut twelve circles from the dough using a 6-inch cutter or using a knife and a 6-inch bowl as a guide, or just cut large squares from the sheet using a very sharp knife.

3. Place a small amount of the filling in the center of six of the dough circles. Then make a small well in the center of each mound of filling. Gently place an egg yolk into each well. Carefully cover each with a second circle of dough and seal the edges with a little water, crimping them firmly together.

4. Bring a large pot of salted water to a rolling boil. Very gently lower the ravioli into the water one at a time with a slotted spoon and cook for 2 minutes.

5. Meanwhile, melt the butter in a sauté pan. When the ravioli are cooked, gently remove them from the water with a slotted spoon, place them in the sauté pan, and coat with the butter. Serve each one on a small plate generously sprinkled with grated Parmigiano.

STANLEY'S TIP

You may have some dough left after making your ravioli—in this case, either put the dough through your pasta machine on a fettuccine setting or just coarsely slice the remaining pasta to create *malfatti*, or "misshapen" pasta. Hang the strands on a pasta rack or over some wooden spoons balanced over large pots to dry thoroughly. Then store in zip-top bags or airtight storage containers until needed.

trofiette with pesto genovese, string beans, and potatoes

Serves 4 to 6

1 large russet potato, peeled

1 pound trofiette pasta

4 ounces string beans, cut into thirds

1 cup Pesto Sauce (page 215)

Extra virgin olive oil, for serving

Freshly grated Parmigiano-Reggiano, for serving

This recipe is from my dear friend Camilla Toniolo, a very talented film editor who cut *Blind Date*, a film I directed a number of years ago. Cooking is her other love, and she's equally brilliant at it. We edited the film in my home and happily spent equal amounts of time working, cooking, and eating together. If you can't find the trofiette, use ziti or penne instead.

---

1. In a large pot, bring 6 quarts of well-salted water to a rolling boil.

2. Cut the potato into 1-inch cubes, submerging the cubes in water as you work so that they don't discolor.

3. Add the pasta, potato, and string beans to the pot. Cook until the pasta is al dente and the potato and beans are soft and cooked through, about 20 minutes.

4. Pour the pesto into a large serving bowl. Drain the pasta and vegetables, saving half the pasta cooking water. Slowly add the water to the pesto in the bowl, stirring to loosen it until the pesto is creamy but not watery. Add the pasta and vegetables to the sauce, toss them together, drizzle with extra virgin olive oil, and serve with freshly grated Parmigiano.

pasta al forno
baked pasta

When I'm making pasta for the kids, I'll often cook an extra pound and double the marinara so I can make this dish the next day. I often have pesto on hand, as it keeps really well in the fridge as long as it's topped off with oil. This is something I make for them on a Friday or Saturday night when they have friends sleep over. It gives me great joy to watch them all devour it as though they haven't eaten for weeks.

If you're cooking pasta specifically for this dish, cook it very al dente and let it finish cooking in the oven. Just make sure you coat your extra pasta with a little olive oil to stop it sticking together before you store it in the fridge.

———————

1. Preheat the oven to 350°F.

2. Briefly blend the marinara sauce with an immersion blender—for this dish, it helps if it is smoother than normal.

3. Mix the sauces, pasta, and Parmigiano together in a baking dish and season with salt and pepper. Cover the baking dish with aluminum foil and bake for 30 to 40 minutes, lifting the foil and stirring occasionally. Remove the foil for the last few minutes of cooking to just bubble and crisp the top.

Serves 4 to 6

4 cups Marinara Sauce (page 216)

½ to ¾ cup Pesto Sauce (page 215)

2 to 3 cups Béchamel Sauce (page 217)

1 pound cooked ziti or penne

1 to 1½ cups freshly grated Parmigiano-Reggiano

Kosher salt and freshly ground black pepper

gnocchi with sage butter

Serves 4

FOR THE GNOCCHI

1½ pounds floury potatoes, i.e. russet, unpeeled

1 egg, lightly beaten

1 egg yolk, lightly beaten

2 teaspoons olive oil

1 teaspoon kosher salt

¾ to 1 cup flour, as needed

1 cup freshly grated Parmigiano-Reggiano, plus more for serving

FOR THE SAUCE

8 tablespoons (1 stick) butter

10 fresh sage leaves

Freshly ground black pepper

Felicity says: "The key to making gnocchi is to make sure you have the right potatoes—the most floury potatoes you can find to keep your gnocchi light and the dough easy to manipulate. With a waxy potato, you'll end up with an immovable, gloopy mess at the end."

Here, we're using a simple sauce of butter and sage. But gnocchi's great with Marinara Sauce (page 216) or Pesto Sauce (page 215), or with just some butter and cheese.

———————

1. Make the gnocchi: Put the potatoes in a medium saucepan with enough cold water to cover and season with a good pinch of salt. Bring the water to a low boil and cook the potatoes until very tender but not breaking apart, making sure that they are completely cooked, which takes about 20 minutes.

2. Remove the potatoes from the water and spread them on a baking sheet. Split them in two to release their steam. (This allows more water to evaporate and will make them easier to work with, and render your gnocchi fluffier.) When they are cool enough to handle, gently peel off the skins, place the flesh in a bowl, and mash well, preferably by running the flesh through a potato ricer. Spread the potato on your work surface and leave it to cool completely.

3. Gather the cooled potatoes into a mound and make a well in the center. Place the egg and the olive oil in the well. Season with salt. Then place ¾ cup of the flour and the Parmigiano around the outside of the potato circle and, using a fork, gradually mix all the ingredients into the potato to form a smooth dough. The amount of flour varies depending on the potato, so you may need to add a little more as you go. Once it has come together, knead the dough for 4 to 5 minutes, just to work the flour through. Form the dough into a short, fat sausage shape.

4. Bring a large pot of salted water to a boil. If you will not be serving the gnocchi right away, set up a bowl full of ice water near the stove.

5. Lightly flour a clean work surface and cut the dough into quarters. Roll each quarter into a longer sausage shape about ½ inch in diameter.

6. Now, the easier method is to go along the lines of dough, pinching it every half inch or so, and then cut off each gnocchi with a sharp knife so you have lots of small pillow shapes. If you are feeling more confident, cut the lines of gnocchi into ½-inch slices, shaping them with your thumb and rolling them down the back of a fork so that each one has an indentation on one side and a few sauce-holding grooves on the other.

7. Cook the gnocchi in batches in the boiling water. They will sink at first, then rise to the top when they are cooked. You can now either cook the gnocchi in their sauce and serve, or refrigerate them to serve later. If you will be eating them right away, remove them with a slotted spoon and set aside in a warm serving dish. If you are not serving them right away, remove them with a slotted spoon and immediately place them in the bowl of ice water to cool, then transfer to an airtight container and refrigerate. Repeat until all the gnocchi are cooked.

8. Make the sauce: In a sauté pan, gently melt the butter. Add the sage leaves and allow them to cook for a minute to infuse the butter with flavor. Toss the gnocchi in the sauce to really coat them, season with additional Parmigiano and freshly ground black pepper, and serve at once.

FELICITY'S TIP

If you are short on time, don't worry about the forking step. Just pinch the dough and cut, pinch the dough and cut. You'll get lovely half-smiles that look great.

basic risotto

Serves 4 to 6

1½ quarts good chicken or vegetable stock

3 to 4 tablespoons butter

1 large shallot, finely chopped

½ onion, finely chopped

3 cups risotto rice

5 ounces dry white wine

Kosher salt and freshly ground black pepper

1 cup freshly grated Parmigiano-Reggiano

There's no doubt that the process of making risotto is a time-consuming and delicate one, however, as we all know, the results are well worth it.

This is a basic plain risotto recipe, but I have included options in the Tips for making saffron and lemon versions.

The first tip below was taught to me many years ago by my friend Gianni Scappin, and it's the method used in most restaurants across the world. It allows you to still make a delicious risotto but spend more time with your guests.

I prefer Vialone Nano rice from Italy's Po Valley, which is the traditional rice of the Veneto.

———————

1. Bring the stock to a simmer in a large saucepan and keep it simmering gently within easy reach.

2. In a separate, medium-sized Dutch oven, melt 2 tablespoons of the butter over medium heat. Add the shallot and onion and cook gently for about 5 minutes, until they are soft and translucent. Add the rice and stir to combine it with the butter, shallot, and onion, coating and toasting each grain thoroughly. Cook for 2 minutes more, then add the wine, stirring it into the rice. Keep stirring until the wine has been almost completely absorbed.

3. Now add the first ladle of stock—enough to just cover the rice—and season with salt, then reduce the heat a little. Keep stirring often so that the rice doesn't stick. (Note: You don't want the heat turned down too low, or your rice will become chalky, or turned up too high, where it becomes gummy. As you do this more often, you will learn to feel how much you need to stir, and how and when to adjust the temperature.)

recipe continued on next page

4. Keep adding the stock as the rice absorbs it, a ladle at a time and then in decreasing quantities, until the rice is cooked, stirring gently and continuously throughout. It should take about 20 minutes, sometimes a little longer, depending on the rice. When it's done, the rice grains should be al dente and the risotto itself should have a creamy, giving texture. It should not be wet.

5. Remove the risotto from the heat and season with salt and pepper. Then add the remaining 1 to 2 tablespoons butter and the Parmigiano and stir well to combine. Serve immediately.

STANLEY'S TIPS

• To precook a risotto, follow the recipe exactly as above, but stop cooking after you've been adding the stock for 10 to 13 minutes. Spread the rice out on a marble slab or a baking sheet. Set it aside to cool or refrigerate it. When you're ready to cook it, bring the stock back to the simmer, return the rice to its pan, and cook as above until it reaches the right consistency.

• I prefer to use a silicone spatula as it is gentle on the rice.

• To make lemon risotto, add ½ tablespoon freshly squeezed lemon juice about halfway through the cooking process, and ½ teaspoon lemon zest can be added at the end with the Parmigiano and butter.

• To make saffron risotto, add a pinch of saffron to your stock at the beginning to dissolve before adding the stock to the rice.

• If you have leftover risotto, use it to make Risotto Cakes (page 36).

israeli couscous with slow-roasted tomatoes and caramelized onions

Couscous is essentially pasta with North African origins. This Israeli couscous has a large pearl shape and feels delightful when you bite into it. The just-tender pasta, the sweet, almost jammy roasted tomatoes, and the caramelized onions are a match made in heaven.

———————

1. In a frying pan, heat the olive oil over medium heat. Add the onions, reduce the heat to medium-low, and slowly cook the onions, stirring occasionally, until they begin to caramelize and become tender and golden brown, about 20 minutes. Remove from the heat and set aside to cool.

2. In a large saucepan, combine 1½ cups of the chicken stock and the saffron and bring to a boil. Add the couscous and reduce the heat to low. Simmer, stirring from time to time as you continue to add the remaining hot stock, ⅓ cup at a time until the couscous is cooked, about 20 minutes. Don't worry if it sticks together—you can always add a little more stock to loosen it. Once the couscous is fully cooked, drain, add the tomatoes and onions, and stir together.

3. Stir the roasted garlic into the couscous. Season with salt and pepper, garnish with the parsley, and serve at room temperature.

Serves 6

¼ cup extra virgin olive oil

1½ yellow onions, sliced lengthwise

2½ cups chicken stock

Pinch of saffron

2 cups Israeli couscous

12 oven-roasted tomatoes (page 170)

1 whole head garlic, roasted (see page 20)

1 tablespoon chopped fresh flat-leaf parsley

Kosher salt and freshly ground black pepper

seafood paella

Serves 10 to 12

FOR THE SOFRITO

1 teaspoon saffron, lightly toasted

4 tablespoons extra virgin olive oil

1 red onion, chopped

1 sweet onion, chopped

1 shallot, finely chopped

3 cloves garlic, chopped

½ red bell pepper, chopped

½ green bell pepper, chopped

One 28-ounce can plum tomatoes, crushed by hand

Kosher salt

1 bay leaf

1 sprig fresh thyme

FOR THE PAELLA

2 pounds jumbo shrimp, shells on

2 tablespoons extra virgin olive oil

1 tablespoon sweet Spanish paprika

1 cup white wine

1 pound bomba rice

PARTY SIZE

A while back, I bought an outdoor paella cooker, which you can fire up with gas, wood, or charcoal. My friends thought I was crazy, until they saw it in action and reaped its benefits. If you happen to have one of these contraptions, follow the recipe immediately below. If you want to make a smaller, stove-top version, we have included a recipe for that as well.

———————

1. First toast the saffron. Wrap the strands in an aluminum foil packet and toast it gently in a dry frying pan or toaster oven for a couple of minutes. This will release the flavor of the saffron.

2. Before preparing the sofrito, peel 1 pound of the shrimp, reserving the shells for a Quick Shrimp Stock (page 210). Set aside the peeled shrimp.

3. In the paella pan, heat the olive oil over medium-high heat. Add the unpeeled shrimp and cook for a couple of minutes, until they are halfway to changing color. Remove and set aside.

4. For the sofrito: In the paella pan, heat the olive oil over low heat. Add the onions and the shallot and cook gently to soften them without allowing them to color. Add the garlic and the bell peppers and cook over low heat until softened. Stir in the toasted saffron and paprika. Add the tomatoes and season generously with salt. Add the bay leaf and thyme and cook it down slowly until the mixture has softened, about 7 to 10 minutes.

5. Raise the heat to medium-high and add the rice and white wine and stir until the alcohol has burned off, about 1 minute. Now add the chicken and shrimp stocks. The stock should completely cover the rice. Spread the ingredients out evenly in the pan and bring to a boil over high heat, until the rice rises to the surface of the liquid, about 5 minutes. Reduce the heat to medium-low and simmer for 15 to 20 minutes more. Do not stir. Add the clams, mussels, and all of the shrimp. Spread them out evenly in the paella, never stirring, and continue cooking until the shellfish have opened, about 5 minutes or so. Remove from the heat and let the paella rest for a few minutes before serving.

6. If, at this point, the rice is looking a bit damp, raise the heat for a few minutes to evaporate the liquid. Ideally, the rice will now have a lovely golden crust on the bottom, which the Spanish call a *socarrat*. Remove from the heat and serve.

Note: Make sure to check through the shellfish when you're cleaning them, and discard any that have broken shells or fail to close when you tap their shells firmly.

STANLEY'S TIP

For those who aren't keen on just seafood, you can adapt this recipe by adding chicken. Take 6 chicken thighs, season with salt and pepper, and sauté them in a separate pan, skin-down, in olive oil until the skin is crispy, approximately 7 minutes. Turn them over to cook through and set aside. Add them to the paella after the rice has cooked for 5 minutes. Distribute them evenly throughout the pan, pushing them down into the rice.

3 to 4 cups Chicken Stock (page 208)

3 cups Quick Shrimp Stock (page 210)

2 pounds clams, cleaned (see Note)

2 pounds mussels, cleaned and debearded (see Note)

recipe pictured on next page

paella

Serves 4

FOR THE SOFRITO

2 tablespoons extra virgin olive oil

½ red onion, chopped

½ sweet onion, chopped

½ shallot, finely chopped

2 cloves garlic, chopped

¼ red bell pepper, chopped

¼ green bell pepper, chopped

½ teaspoon saffron, lightly toasted (see Step 1, page 72)

One 7-ounce can plum tomatoes, crushed by hand

1 bay leaf

Kosher salt

FOR THE PAELLA

½ pound jumbo shrimp

1 tablespoon extra virgin olive oil

½ pound bomba rice

1 teaspoon sweet Spanish smoked paprika

½ cup white wine

1½ cups Chicken Stock (page 208)

1½ cups seafood stock (page 210)

½ pound clams, cleaned (see Note, page 73)

½ pound mussels, cleaned and debearded (see Note, page 73)

STOVETOP VERSION

This version calls for a 13½-inch paella pan.

———————

1. Peel half of the shrimp and set aside. In the paella pan, heat the olive oil over medium heat. Add the unpeeled shrimp and cook for a couple of minutes until they are halfway to changing color. Set aside.

2. For the sofrito: In the paella pan, heat the olive oil over low heat. Add the onions and the shallot and cook gently to soften them without allowing them to color. Add the garlic and the bell peppers and cook over low heat until softened. Stir in the toasted saffron and paprika. Add the tomatoes and the bay leaf, and season generously with salt. Cook until the mixture has softened, about 7 to 10 minutes.

3. Raise the heat to medium-high and add the rice and the white wine. Stir everything all together until the alcohol has burned off. Add the chicken and seafood stocks and bring to a boil. Lower the heat to a simmer, spread the ingredients out evenly in the pan, and cook for about 15 minutes without stirring, until the rice has absorbed a lot of the liquid. Add the clams, mussels, and all of the shrimp, never stirring, and continue cooking until the shellfish opened, about 5 to 10 minutes.

4. If, at this point, the rice is looking a bit damp, raise the heat for a few minutes to evaporate the liquid. Ideally, the rice will now have a lovely golden crust on the bottom, which the Spanish call a *socarrat*. Remove from the heat and serve.

Note: If you wish to add chicken, see the tip on page 73, but only use 4 thighs.

fish and seafood

"After immigrating to America my mother's family settled in Verplanck, New York, a small town on the Hudson River. In the back of their modest house was a sizable garden in which they not only grew everything imaginable, but where they raised rabbits, chickens, and the occasional goat or two; all of which were used to sustain a growing family. Being so near the river, they were also able to cull its edible riches to add to their table. As a boy, I loved going to the Hudson with my grandparents, tying pieces of raw chicken to the bottom of crab nets and lowering them off the end of an abandoned steamboat dock into the river's green-brown waters. By late afternoon we would be devouring a bevy of boiled crabs accompanied by corn on the cob, boiled potatoes, tomato salad, and my grandmother's homemade bread. The feast was served on a newspaper-covered table nestled beneath a grapevine-wrapped trellis. If my uncle Tony and aunt Grace had recently returned from Cape Cod, we would be treated to their catch of fresh clams on the half shell and bluefish. All of this followed by a boisterous game of bocce made for what are now much-missed seafood-filled summer days."

—Stanley

camilla toniolo's whole baked fish with sliced potatoes

Serves 4

⅓ cup olive oil

6 medium to large red potatoes (about 2 pounds), peeled and very thinly sliced

5 sprigs fresh rosemary

2 bay leaves

2 cloves garlic, chopped

Kosher salt

Freshly ground black pepper

1 large pompano, sea bass, grouper, or red snapper

Juice of 1 lemon

⅓ cup white wine

This is another recipe from my friend Camilla Toniolo (page 62). I love the creaminess of the potatoes and how they soak up the flavor of the fish. She makes it with pompano, but other fish, such as grouper, red snapper, and sea bass, can be substituted.

———————

1. Preheat the oven to 400°F.

2. Drizzle half the olive oil into a large roasting pan. Then place the potatoes evenly across the pan, tossing them so they are coated with the oil. Add 4 sprigs of the rosemary, the bay leaves, and the garlic, layering them between the potatoes, and season with salt and pepper. Bake for about 20 minutes.

3. Meanwhile, season the inside of the pompano with salt and half the lemon juice, and stuff it with the remaining sprig of rosemary. Squeeze the rest of the lemon over the outside of the fish and sprinkle with salt.

4. Remove the potatoes from the oven, place the fish directly on top of them, and pour the remaining oil and the wine over the fish. Bake for 35 to 45 minutes, or until the fish is flaking and the potatoes are tender and brown at the edges. The fish is cooked when the thickest part near the head flakes easily while inserting a fork. To fillet the fish remove the dorsal bones with a spatula first, then cut down the middle of the fish and move the top and bottom fillets to a serving platter. Remove the middle bone and the head in one piece pulling from the tail and discard. Add to platter and scoop the potatoes around the fish fillets. Garnish with lemon wedges and sprinkle some raw olive oil and salt on the fillets if you want.

CAMILLA'S TIP

If Camilla is cooking two or three smaller fish, she will leave the potatoes in the oven to cook a little longer, as the fish will take less time and you want the potatoes to be cooked through.

Note: You can mix potatoes and Jerusalem artichokes (sunchokes) if you like them.

baked salmon

I don't think you need to do a lot to salmon to make it taste great. This makes a delicious light supper. Any leftovers can be served the next day with a green salad for a light lunch.

——————————

1. Preheat the oven to 350°F.

2. Rub the oil over the fish and across the bottom of a roasting pan. Place the fish in the pan, skin-side down, and add the scallions, garlic, and wine. Season with salt and pepper. Cover the pan with aluminum foil and bake for 10 minutes. Uncover the pan and bake for 2 minutes or so more. The fish should be nicely medium rare.

Serves 4

1 tablespoon olive oil

4 salmon fillets

3 to 4 scallions, trimmed and halved lengthwise

1 clove garlic, coarsely sliced

2 tablespoons white wine

Kosher salt and freshly ground black pepper

steamed trout
with court bouillon sauce

Trout is a delicious and less expensive alternative to salmon. It's often pan-fried, but I prefer this more delicate cooking method, which effectively steams the fish over a light bouillon. Adding butter at the end gives the sauce a delicate richness.

————————

1. Place the water, wine, parsley, thyme, bay leaf, lemon, salt, peppercorns, garlic, leek, and carrot in a large saucepan or a steamer. Bring to a boil, cover, and simmer for 10 minutes. Place the fish on a rack over the top, cover tightly with aluminum foil, and simmer for 12 to 15 minutes more. If you are using a fish poacher or steamer, just prop the rack up with a couple of heatproof ramekins.

2. Remove the rack and set the fish aside to keep warm.

3. Strain the court bouillon into a small saucepan, setting aside the carrots and leeks, and cook over medium-high heat until it has reduced by about a third. Add the butter, stirring it in to create an emulsified sauce. Return the carrots and leeks to the sauce, taste, and adjust the seasoning if necessary.

4. Gently peel the skin from the trout and carefully divide the fillets among four plates. Spoon the sauce over each portion, making sure to include some pieces of leek and carrot, and garnish with a little fresh chervil.

5. Serve immediately.

Serves 4

2 cups water

1 cup wine

Few sprigs fresh flat-leaf parsley

Few sprigs fresh thyme

1 bay leaf

1 slice lemon

Good pinch of kosher salt

½ teaspoon whole black peppercorns

1 clove garlic, smashed

½ leek, thickly sliced

½ carrot, thickly sliced

Two 12-ounce rainbow trout, cleaned and gutted, heads and tails on

2 tablespoons butter

1 tablespoon chopped fresh chervil or flat-leaf parsley

roasted sea bass

Serves 2 to 4

1 whole medium sea bass, gutted and scaled, head and tail on

Kosher salt and freshly ground black pepper

1 to 2 cloves garlic, sliced

¼ lemon, cut into semicircular slices

2 sprigs fresh rosemary

2 sprigs fresh thyme

2 sprigs fresh flat-leaf parsley

6 tablespoons extra virgin olive oil

6 to 8 whole cherry tomatoes

½ cup dry white wine

This is a classic branzino recipe that you will pay a lot for in restaurants but is so quick and easy to do yourself. Cooking the whole fish like this gives the flesh so much more flavor and makes for a beautiful presentation. Don't be intimidated by the idea of filleting it, as you can easily lift the flesh off the spine to serve. This is my fish-loving daughter Camilla's favorite.

———————

1. Preheat the oven to 425°F.

2. Season the cavity of the fish with salt and pepper, then stuff it with the garlic, lemon, herbs, and 3 tablespoons of the olive oil.

3. Rub the skin of the fish with the remaining 3 tablespoons oil, place it in a roasting pan, add the tomatoes, and pour in the white wine. Season with salt and pepper. Roast for 15 to 20 minutes, gently turning the fish once, until the skin blisters and the flesh comes away from the bone.

cod baked with tomatoes and olives

Serves 4 to 6

4 tablespoons extra virgin olive oil

1 medium onion, chopped

1 to 2 cloves garlic, chopped

Kosher salt

One 14-ounce can whole San Marzano tomatoes, crushed by hand

1 bay leaf

3 ounces good quality black olives

Freshly ground black pepper

4 to 6 cod fillets (5 to 6 ounces each), skinned

1 tablespoon chopped fresh flat-leaf parsley

This *merluzzo al forno* is a version of a classic Livornese dish. You can make it with any firm, white fish, like red snapper or halibut, but I like it best with cod. Capers can be added for more acidity.

———

1. In a saucepan, heat 3 tablespoons of the olive oil over medium heat. Add the onion and the garlic and cook until soft but not colored, 5 to 7 minutes. Add a little salt and stir through until the mixture is well coated with the oil and onions. Meanwhile, crush the tomatoes in a bowl with your hands. Add them to the saucepan, together with the bay leaf and salt. Stir everything together, bring to a boil, and then reduce the heat to a simmer and cook for 15 to 20 minutes. Stir in the olives, remove from the heat, and season with salt and pepper.

2. Preheat the oven to 350°F.

3. Spoon a thin layer of the sauce into a baking dish. Then lay the fish on top and spoon the remaining sauce over the top. Make sure all the fish has at least a light covering of sauce. Drizzle with the remaining 1 tablespoon olive oil, cover with aluminium foil, and bake for 15 to 20 minutes, until the fish is almost cooked through. Remove from the oven and allow to rest so that the fish keeps cooking in the sauce's residual heat and remains moist. Garnish with the parsley and serve.

grilled sardines with salsa verde

People are so used to canned sardines that I think they forget how delicious a freshly grilled sardine can be. They're crispy, oily, and a taste of the sea. These are reminiscent of the fresh fish we had cooked on a beachside barbecue in Portugal on one of the first vacations Felicity, the kids, and I had together.

Serve them with the salsa verde below.

———————

1. Make the sardines: In a small heavy-bottomed frying pan, gently heat ½ cup of the olive oil over low heat. Add the garlic and basil and cook very gently to infuse the oil with their flavor, about 1 minute. Do not allow the garlic to color, or the basil to crisp. Remove the pan from the heat and set aside to cool. Then strain, discarding the garlic and basil.

2. Rub the sardines with the remaining oil and season them inside and out with salt and pepper. Heat a griddle or grill to an even medium heat and grill the sardines for 3 to 5 minutes a side, until the skin is crisp and the flesh is cooked through.

3. Place the fish on a serving plate and dress them with the garlic-basil oil. You don't have to use all the oil here. Sprinkle with the parsley and an extra grind or two of black pepper.

4. Make the salsa verde: In a food processor or using a mortar and pestle, grind the garlic and anchovies together. Then add the herbs. If you're using a food processor, add them carefully—I like to retain a little of their texture, but follow your preference. Squeeze in the lemon juice and stir it in along with the capers (if using). Season thoroughly with pepper, then add olive oil to taste, to create a cohesive and balanced sauce. If you need to add salt, add salt. This will keep for no more than a day.

5. Serve the sardines with the salsa verde alongside.

Serves 4 to 6

FOR THE SARDINES

⅔ cup extra virgin olive oil

3 cloves garlic, finely chopped

4 fresh basil leaves, torn

8 to 12 sardines

1 teaspoon salt

Freshly ground black pepper

¼ cup coarsely chopped fresh flat-leaf parsley

FOR THE SALSA VERDE

2 to 3 cloves garlic

One 2-ounce can anchovies

Handful of fresh basil

Handful of fresh mint

Handful of fresh flat-leaf parsley

Lemon juice, to taste

1 tablespoon capers, rinsed (optional)

Freshly ground black pepper

Olive oil

Kosher salt (optional)

fish stew

Serves 4 to 6

3 tablespoons olive oil

1 large onion, diced

1 large shallot, finely diced

1 to 2 large cloves garlic, minced

1 to 2 dried pepperoncini

Pinch of saffron

¾ cup dry white wine

2 cups chopped fresh tomatoes

3 fresh basil leaves

4 cups Fish Stock (page 210), hot

Kosher salt and freshly ground black pepper

6 scallops

10 ounces cod, cut into 3-inch cubes

10 ounces grouper, cut into 3-inch cubes

12 clams

12 mussels

12 large shrimp, tails left on

1 tablespoon chopped fresh flat-leaf parsley

Toasted baguette, for serving

Extra virgin olive oil, for serving

I love fish. I love stew. I *love* fish stew. This version—*stufato di pesce*—is Italian in origin, but I have added a little saffron as an homage to a French bouillabaisse.

———————

In a large Dutch oven, heat the olive oil over medium-high heat. Add the onion, shallot, garlic, peperoncini, and saffron and cook for 3 to 5 minutes until softened. Add the white wine, raise the heat to high, and cook until the alcohol has burned off. Lower the heat to medium-high, add the tomatoes, basil, salt, and pepper, and cook for 5 minutes more. Reduce the heat to medium, and add the stock. Stir the mixture together and bring to a low bubble. (If you worry that the fish stock is too fishy, you can add some chicken broth.) Add the scallops, cod, and grouper to the pot and simmer, covered, for 5 to 7 minutes. Do not stir. Then add the clams and mussels and cover the pot again. Once they begin to open, add the shrimp. Simmer until the shrimp turn pink. Add the parsley and serve immediately with some of the toasted baguette drizzled with a touch of extra virgin olive oil.

fish and chips

Serves 4

FOR THE CHIPS

2 pounds large potatoes, peeled and cut into ½-inch-thick pieces

Vegetable oil, for deep-frying

Kosher salt

FOR THE BEER-BATTERED FISH

2½ cups all-purpose flour, chilled

2 teaspoons baking powder

2 cups beer, chilled

½ to 1 teaspoon kosher salt

4 cod or haddock steaks (5 to 6 ounces each), no more than 1-inch thick

TO SERVE

Kosher salt

Malt vinegar

Felicity's earliest memory of eating fish and chips is with her sister, Emily, and their Nanna. Felicity says, "On the way back from the pictures, we would stop off at the local fish-and-chip shop and get huge pieces of deep-fried cod and all sorts of odd-shaped chips cooked in beef drippings. They were served in newspaper and doused generously with malt vinegar and table salt. You had the option of ordering mushy peas on the side, which we never did, but now I always make some to go with this. We would carry the slightly steaming parcels home as quickly as we could. The sheer excitement of unwrapping them when we got there still resonates with me all these years later."

––––––––––––

1. Make the chips: Soak the potatoes in a bowl of cold water for an hour or so, or just run them under cold running water if you are short on time. This will help remove some of the starches from them. Dry thoroughly.

2. Heat the oil to 190°F. Working in batches, blanch the chips in the oil for 8 to 12 minutes, until they are just cooked through. Using a slotted spoon, remove the chips and set aside to drain on paper towels. Let them cool completely. (You can refrigerate them, if you like.) Increase the temperature of the oil to 350°F.

3. Make the beer-battered fish: When the oil comes to temperature, make the cold beer batter: Sift the chilled flour and the baking powder together in a bowl, then whisk in the cold beer and the salt until really smooth. Dip the fish into the cold batter so that it's well coated and allow any excess to drip off. Then fry the fish in the hot oil for 5 to 8 minutes, until crisp and golden. Make sure you cook only 1 or 2 pieces of fish at a time, or you will reduce the oil temperature. Make sure that you shake the basket as soon as the battered fish goes in, as this will keep the fish from sticking.

4. Remove the fish and drain on paper towels while you finish the chips.

5. Allow the oil to come back to temperature, and then fry the chips, working in batches, for 2 to 3 minutes, until they're crispy and golden. Remove and drain on paper towels. Season with salt.

6. Portion everything out onto plates, and serve with salt and malt vinegar on the side.

FELICITY'S TIP

• Make sure all the ingredients for the batter are really cold. This means refrigerate the flour for 30 minutes or so, as well as the beer, before mixing them.

• For the chips, choose a good floury potato to ensure fluffy chips. If you want to serve it with our version of mushy peas, simply follow the pea puree instructions on page 99, adding a little of the peas' cooking water as you reheat it.

steamed mussels

Serves 2 to 4

2 pounds mussels, cleaned and debearded

Good pinch of saffron

1 cup white wine

3 tablespoons extra virgin olive oil, plus more for serving

2 cloves garlic, finely chopped

1 shallot, finely diced

1 cup finely sliced leeks

6 cherry tomatoes, halved

1 cup water

Kosher salt and freshly ground black pepper

1 tablespoon chopped fresh flat-leaf parsley, plus more for serving

Mussels are inexpensive, plentiful, and delicious. I remember going kayaking years ago to gather mussels and ending up with a five-gallon drum of them. I prepared them like this, fresh out of the cold Maine waters.

————————

1. Discard any mussels that are broken or remain open even when tapped on the shell with your fingernail.

2. Mix the saffron into the wine and set aside.

3. In a large, deep pot, heat the olive oil over medium-low heat. Add the garlic and cook, stirring, without allowing it to color. Add the shallot and leeks and stir to coat well with the oil. Cook until they have softened and wilted but have not taken any color. Raise the heat to medium-high, add the wine mixture, and allow the alcohol to burn off, then add the tomatoes and mix well. Reduce the heat to medium and add the water. Now add the mussels. Season with a couple of good pinches of salt and pepper and the parsley. Stir to coat. Cover and cook for 3 to 6 minutes, shaking the pan every now and then. The dish is done when all the mussels have opened. Finish with a good drizzle of extra virgin olive oil and more parsley, if you wish. See finished dish on page 80.

seared scallops with pea puree

This combination of flavors: sweet, succulent scallops, salty prosciutto, and earthy peas looks stunning and is very simple to make.

———————

1. Make the puree: Bring a saucepan of salted water to a rolling boil. Cook the peas until they're just tender, 3 to 4 minutes. Strain them in a colander, reserving about ½ cup of their cooking water. Put the peas in a blender with the olive oil, salt and pepper to taste, and a touch of the reserved cooking water, and blend until smooth. You're looking for a creamy consistency. Feel free to leave a little texture if you prefer. You can make this well ahead of time, so set it aside with the rest of the reserved pea cooking water until needed. Otherwise, keep the puree warm in a small saucepan. If it gets too thick, loosen it with a couple of tablespoons of the reserved cooking water.

2. Make the scallops: Preheat the oven to 350°F. Line a baking sheet with aluminum foil and lay the prosciutto on top. Lay a second sheet of foil on top of the prosciutto, and then set a second baking sheet on top. This will ensure that the prosciutto stays flat as it cooks. Bake for 10 to 15 minutes. Remove and set aside until needed.

3. In a sauté pan, heat the oil and butter over medium-high heat. Add the scallops and cook for 1 minute to 90 seconds on one side, then flip and cook for 30 seconds to 1 minute on the other, basting them frequently with the oil and butter and seasoning them with salt and pepper until they are nicely browned and almost cooked through. Remember, they will keep cooking in their residual heat once you've set them aside.

4. Place 2 to 3 spoonfuls of pea puree on each serving plate. Top it with the scallops, then crumble the crispy prosciutto over the top. Drizzle with a little extra virgin olive oil and garnish with the pea shoots, if desired.

Serves 4

FOR THE PUREE

1 pound peas (thawed, if frozen)

2 tablespoons olive oil

Sea salt and freshly ground black pepper

FOR THE SCALLOPS

4 slices prosciutto

1 tablespoon olive oil

1 tablespoon butter

4 large or 8 smaller scallops (you may have to cut them horizontally in half so that they're about ½-inch thick)

Kosher salt and freshly ground black pepper

Extra virgin olive oil, for drizzling

Pea shoots or micro greens, for garnish (optional)

shrimp with garlic, chile, and parsley

Serves 4

1 pound small to medium shrimp, peeled

3 tablespoons olive oil

2 cloves garlic, thinly sliced

4 whole small peperoncini

Kosher salt and freshly ground black pepper

⅓ cup white wine

1 tablespoon chopped fresh flat-leaf parsley

Lemon wedges, for serving

When I was shooting a film in Majorca, this was a dish I ordered as often as possible. Make sure you get the sauté pan as hot as you dare, so that the shrimp cook fast and remain juicy and sweet.

———————

1. In a large bowl, toss the shrimp together with 2 tablespoons of the olive oil, the garlic, and the peperoncini. Set aside to marinate for 15 to 20 minutes at room temperature.

2. Heat a large sauté pan over high heat until very hot. Add the remaining 1 tablespoon olive oil, then cook the shrimp in batches with their marinade, seasoning them with salt and pepper as you cook them and setting them aside as you go, until they are all pink and done.

3. Deglaze the pan with the white wine, scraping up any cooking residue from the bottom, and stir in the parsley. Pour this pan sauce over the shrimp and serve immediately with lemon wedges.

STANLEY'S TIP

Alternatively, marinate the shrimp in their shells, then put them on skewers and grill over medium-high heat until they are pink and the shells are slightly charred.

meat and fowl

"Soon after we started dating, I asked Felicity what she would like to cook for a dinner party we were having that weekend, and without a moment's pause she exclaimed: 'Suckling pig!' Of course I had never cooked one before and, as it turned out, neither had she. That week we tracked one down at one of the few remaining butchers nearby. Unfortunately, when we got the pig home it was too long to fit on the spit of our barbecue. We had but one option. . . . Needless to say, when the kids came home from school they found us trying to decapitate the carcass of a pig with a hacksaw. Luckily, they have all made complete recoveries. Except for the pig."

—Stanley

standing rib of beef

Serves 8 to 10

FOR THE ROAST BEEF

One 8- to 9-pound fore rib or prime rib of beef (a good 3 to 4 ribs' worth)

½ tablespoon olive oil

1 tablespoon Colman's mustard powder

Kosher salt and freshly ground black pepper

FOR THE GRAVY

1 tablespoon all-purpose flour

1 cup red wine

1 cup beef stock

1 bay leaf

Couple of sprigs fresh thyme

Dash of Worcestershire sauce (optional)

Dash of Angostura bitters (optional)

Kosher salt and freshly ground black pepper (optional)

Felicity's dad, Oliver, makes the most incredible roast beef. He does prefer it on the rare side, so there have been occasions where he's had to be convinced by the rest of the family to take it back to the kitchen and cook it a bit further.

This beef, together with the gravy (recipe below), the Yorkshire Pudding (page 168), English Roast Potatoes (page 164), and a vegetable side of your choosing form a classic English Sunday roast—one of the best meals you'll ever eat.

———————

1. Make the roast beef: Preheat the oven to 425°F.

2. Place the beef in a large roasting pan, fat side up. Rub the oil well into the fat, followed by the mustard powder, and season thoroughly with salt and pepper.

3. Roast the beef for 30 minutes, then reduce the oven temperature to 350°F and roast, basting occasionally, for 12 to 15 minutes more per pound for a medium-rare joint. Note that when you turn down the heat, it's a good idea to open the oven door for a good 30 seconds or so to let some of the extra heat escape.

4. When the meat is cooked to your liking (see Tip, next page), transfer to carving dish to rest for at least 30 minutes before carving.

5. Make the gravy: Spoon all but 1 tablespoon of the beef drippings out of the pan. (You can keep the rest of the drippings for another use or dispose of them, as you wish.)

6. Place the roasting pan on the stove top over medium-high heat. When the fat is hot, add the flour. Cook the flour in the fat until it turns a light brown—a couple of minutes or so. Then add the wine. Stir vigorously to make sure there are no floury lumps, then stir in the stock. Add the bay leaf, thyme, Worcestershire sauce, and bitters (if using), and bring to a boil. Reduce the heat to maintain a simmer and cook until the gravy has reduced and is thick enough to coat the back of a spoon. Add any juices from the rested rib of beef and stir them into the gravy. If you want to add a little more liquid, you can put in some of the vegetable cooking water. Note that this will thin the gravy, so you may want to reduce it a little more. Taste, and season with salt and pepper if necessary.

7. Serve with Yorkshire Pudding (page 168), English Roast Potatoes (page 164), and your favorite vegetables.

STANLEY'S TIPS

• If you're cooking this dish, it's bound to be a special occasion. So it's a good idea to invest in a meat thermometer, if you haven't already, to make sure it's prepared just how you like it. Rare roast beef should have an internal temperature of 120 to 125°F; medium-rare should be 130 to 135°F; medium should be 140 to 145°F; medium-well should be 150 to 155°F.

• For extra-special gravy, add 2 unpeeled shallots to the roasting pan an hour before the beef is ready. When the meat is done, remove the shallots from the pan and remove their skins, then mash them and stir them into the gravy as it reduces.

beef wellington

Serves 6

2 pounds beef fillet

Kosher salt and freshly ground black pepper

1 to 2 tablespoons olive oil

2 tablespoons extra virgin olive oil

2 tablespoons unsalted butter

9 large flat portobello mushrooms, finely chopped

The leaves from 2 large sprigs fresh thyme

¼ cup Armagnac or brandy

12 slices prosciutto, or as many as are needed to wrap the meat

2 sheets puff pastry

1 egg, lightly beaten

2 tablespoons milk

This is another classic British recipe—a crumbly, flaky pastry wrapped around prime beef. Most of the preparation is done ahead of time and then the dish is refrigerated before being popped into the oven, and the result is bit of a showstopper.

––––––––––

1. Preheat the oven to 400°F (this is optional—see step 8).

2. Before cooking, make sure you take the fillet out of the fridge and let it come to room temperature. Season the fillet with salt and pepper.

3. In a large sauté pan, heat the olive oil over medium-high heat. Add the beef and sear it on all sides until it is nicely browned. If you want your beef Wellington medium-rare, set it aside to rest now. If you would like it medium, place it in the oven for 10 minutes, then remove it and set aside to cool before you place it in the refrigerator. You can do this ahead of time.

4. In a large sauté pan, heat the extra virgin olive oil and the butter over medium-low heat. Add the mushrooms with the thyme and cook until the mushrooms are soft and all their water has evaporated, a good 8 to 10 minutes. Then add the Armagnac and continue to cook down, being very careful that the alcohol does not catch fire. Season with salt and pepper to taste and set aside to cool.

5. Lay out a piece of plastic wrap on your work surface and then place another piece across the first to form a cross. Then take the prosciutto slices and lay them out on top in two rows, making sure to lay the prosciutto in the same direction as the top layer of plastic wrap. Make sure the slices overlap so that there are no gaps and they are wide enough to enclose the fillet.

6. Take two-thirds of the cooled mushroom mixture and place it in the center of the prosciutto along its entire length. Using the back of a tablespoon, push the mixture out to the sides. Place the chilled fillet in the middle of the mushroom mixture and take the remaining mushroom mixture and spoon it across the top of the fillet. Lift the top layer of plastic wrap and pull it up around the sides of the fillet, wrapping it over the mushrooms and prosciutto. Do the same going lengthwise with the bottom layer of plastic wrap. Tighten the plastic around the beef fillet so that it almost forms a sausage and then place in the fridge for 15 minutes or so.

7. No need to grease a baking sheet, just line it with parchment paper. Lay one sheet of puff pastry on your work surface. Cut off one third, roll it out slightly with a rolling pin so it's big enough to accommodate the width and length your fillet, and place it on the prepared baking sheet. Take the fillet from the fridge and carefully remove the plastic wrap. Place it in the center of the sheet of puff pastry. In a small bowl, beat the egg and milk together and gently brush some of the mixture along the edge of the puff pastry. Roll out the remaining pastry and carefully place it over the meat. Make sure it is big enough to hang down over the fillet. With a fork, press down the top layer of pastry onto the bottom layer, crimping them together to seal. Take a sharp knife and decoratively score the top of the pastry, without cutting through it. Then brush the remaining egg and milk mixture over the top of the beef Wellington. Refrigerate for a minimum of 1 hour.

8. Preheat the oven to 350°F.

9. Bake in the middle of the oven for 35 to 40 minutes, until golden brown. Let it rest for 10 to 15 minutes, then cut it into half-inch-thick slices and serve with a vegetable of your choice.

STANLEY'S TIP

You want the beef fillet to be as even a thickness as possible so it cooks uniformly.

recipe pictured on next page

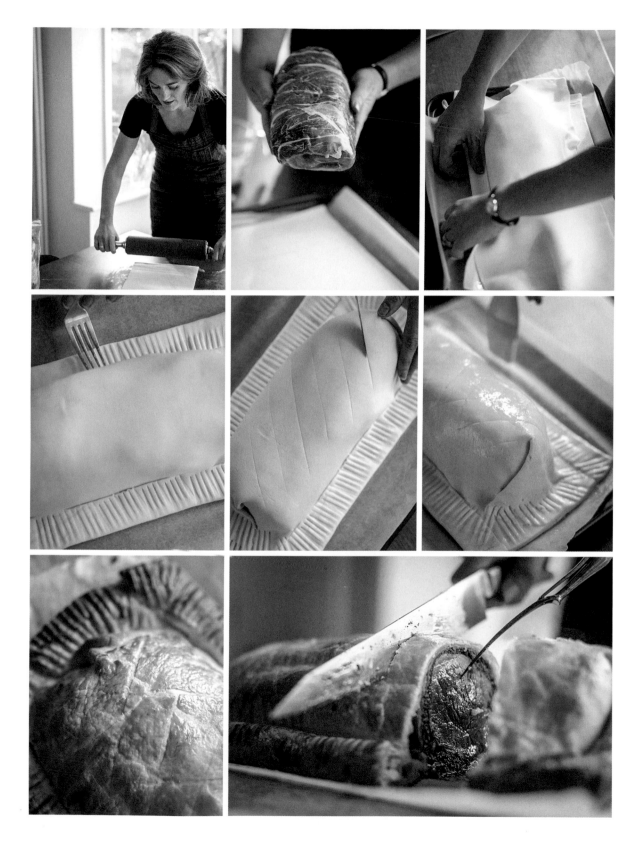

carbonnade de boeuf

Serves 4 to 6

2 to 3 tablespoons flour

Kosher salt and freshly ground black pepper

3 pounds stewing beef, cut into 2-inch cubes

4 to 6 tablespoons olive oil or goose or pork fat

1½ pounds onions (2 to 3 large), thinly sliced

4 cloves garlic, crushed

1¼ pints dark beer, preferably Belgian

2 cups good beef stock

3 tablespoons raw cane sugar

Dash of white wine vinegar

3 bay leaves

Few good sprigs fresh thyme

Small bunch fresh flat-leaf parsley

1 tablespoon Dijon mustard

When I was filming in Brussels, I had this dish at La Brasserie de Bruxelles. I loved it so much that I went again the next night and begged the chef for the recipe. He was kind enough to comply. It is hearty, rustic, and delicious.

———————

1. Preheat the oven to 325°F.

2. Season the flour with salt and pepper and dredge the meat in the seasoned flour.

3. In a heavy-bottomed casserole or Dutch oven, heat the olive oil or goose or pork fat. Add the meat in batches, browning it on all sides, adding some more oil as you go, if necessary. Remove the beef from the pan and set aside. Add the onions to the pan and cook until soft. Add the garlic and cook for a minute or two more. Add half the beer, stirring to deglaze the pan and scraping all the bits off the bottom. Return the meat to the pan and add the remaining beer, the stock, sugar, vinegar, herbs—which you can tie together into a bouquet garni if you like—and the mustard. Stir well and bring to a boil. Cook for a good 5 minutes, then cover and transfer to the oven to bake for about 3 hours, until the meat is tender and the sauce has reduced. Taste the sauce, adjust the seasoning, if necessary, and serve.

STANLEY'S TIPS

• If you feel the sauce needs to be thickened, remove the meat with a slotted spoon, setting it aside on a warm plate, and cook the liquid until it has reduced to your liking. Then return the meat to the pan, heat through, and serve.

• If you prepare this dish twenty-four hours in advance and refrigerate it before reheating, it only adds to its depth of flavor.

steak with oregano, thyme, and rosemary

Serves 6

One 1½- to 2-pound hanger steak, about ¾-inch thick

1 clove garlic, halved

Kosher salt

2 tablespoons olive oil

2 tablespoons butter

Freshly ground black pepper

½ cup red wine

Pinch of chopped fresh rosemary

Leaves from 1 sprig fresh oregano, chopped

Leaves from 2 sprigs fresh thyme, chopped

This is another version of the Steak Oreganata we featured in *The Tucci Cookbook*. It uses hanger steak, which the French call *onglet*. It's quick, easy, inexpensive, and very satisfying. Any leftover steak—cold or reheated—makes a great sandwich the next day.

——————

1. Rub the steak on both sides with the halved garlic and season it with salt. Heat a cast-iron sauté pan over medium-high heat. Add the oil and the butter. When the butter has melted and is foaming rapidly, add the steak. Fry for about 2 to 3 minutes on each side for medium-rare, seasoning with pepper as you go. If overcooked, this particular cut can be quite tough, so be careful. When the steak is done, set it aside on a warm plate. Raise the heat to high and add the wine, rosemary, oregano, and thyme. Cook for a minute or two, scraping any cooking residue from the bottom of the pan. Cut the steak into slices and pour the sauce over the top.

pork chops with onions and mustard

I first had a version of this dish in a little bistro in Paris many years ago, the name of which I can no longer remember. I have tried over the years to re-create what I had that night, and the recipe below is as close as I'll ever get. It may well be Isabel's favorite meal.

———————

1. Season the pork chops all over with salt. In a large sauté pan, heat the olive oil over medium heat. Add the chops and cook for 3 to 4 minutes on each side to brown them. Remove from the sauté pan and set aside.

2. Pour ¼ cup of the wine into the sauté pan and bring to a boil, stirring to deglaze the pan, and scrape up any browned bits from the bottom. Cook for a minute or so to burn off the alcohol, then add the butter. When the butter has melted, add the onion and shallot and cook until they soften. Then add the garlic.

3. Meanwhile, in a large bowl, combine the remaining ½ cup wine, the mustard, mustard seeds, peppercorns, and salt to taste and mix together well. Add this to the sauté pan, along with the chicken stock, thyme, and bay leaf. Return the pork chops to the pan, along with their juices, and cover the pan first with a piece of parchment paper and then with a lid. Simmer for 10 to 15 minutes.

4. Remove the chops from the pan and put them on a warm serving plate. Stir the lemon zest and juice into the sauce and cook over medium-high heat to reduce the sauce by a quarter to a third. Taste and adjust the seasoning. Pour the sauce over the chops and garnish with the parsley.

Serves 4

4 pork chops, on the bone

Kosher salt

2 tablespoons olive oil

¼ cup plus ½ cup dry white wine

2 tablespoons butter

1 large onion, thinly sliced

1 shallot, finely chopped

2 cloves garlic, coarsely sliced

1½ tablespoons Dijon mustard

½ tablespoon mustard seeds, crushed

1 teaspoon dried whole green peppercorns, crushed

1 cup chicken stock

2 sprigs fresh thyme

1 bay leaf

Pinch of lemon zest

2 tablespoons freshly squeezed lemon juice

Good pinch of chopped fresh flat-leaf parsley

roasted pork belly

Serves 6

One 2½- to 3-pound pork belly, skin scored crosswise

¼ cup finely chopped fresh thyme leaves

1½ tablespoons fennel seeds

2 good pinches of kosher salt

1½ tablespoons extra virgin olive oil

2 onions, sliced

3 carrots, halved lengthwise

2 celery stalks, cut into thirds

1 whole head garlic, unpeeled, sliced in half

1¾ cups white wine

1¾ cups chicken stock

1 tablespoon all-purpose flour

Our friend Chef Adam Perry-Lang once arranged for what seemed to be about twenty pounds of pork belly to be delivered to our house one Christmas. Needless to say, we became obsessed with perfecting the ultimate crackling. After a few trials, we found the method below to be consistently successful. However, all of your methods will be for nought unless you have a nice, thick layer of fat on your meat.

By cooking the pork over the roasting vegetables, you end up with a delicious, thick gravy that combines the sweetness integral to the root vegetables with the salty, pork meat juices without you having to do much.

───────────

1. Ideally, take your meat out of the fridge a couple of hours before you want to cook it to bring it to room temperature. This also allows the fat to dry out, making for better crackling.

2. Preheat the oven to 475°F.

3. Place the thyme leaves, fennel seeds, and salt in a mortar and pound them with a pestle. When they are ground, pour in the olive oil and mix until they form a thin paste. Rub the paste into the pork belly skin, working it into the scored skin. The oil will help the herbs stick to the pork. Make sure to rub the paste into the bottom of the belly, too, so it imparts as much flavor as possible to your meat.

4. Place the pork belly on a roasting rack set in a deep baking pan. Roast the pork for about 30 minutes, until the skin has started to puff and turn golden. Remove and distribute the vegetables and garlic underneath the rack. Reduce the oven temperature to 325°F and bake for 1 hour more.

5. Pour half of the wine and half of the stock into the pan and continue to bake for 45 minutes more. Check that your meat is utterly soft, then remove from the oven; otherwise, continue cooking until the meat starts to fall apart. Note that every piece of meat you cook will be a little different—some will have more fat, some a little less. When the meat is done, let it rest for 15 minutes or so while you make the gravy.

6. Remove the rack from the roasting pan and set the pan on the stove top over low heat. Whisk in the flour until the mixture starts to thicken. Add the remaining stock and wine and bring to a simmer while mashing the vegetables into the liquid. Pour the mixture through a sieve into a bowl, pushing on the solids with the back of a spoon; discard any solids left in the sieve and transfer the gravy to a warmed gravy boat.

7. Coarsely chop the pork into pieces of meat and crackling and serve on a board with the gravy on the side.

8. Serve with Mashed Potatoes (page 148) or Basic Risotto (pages 67–68) and roasted vegetables. To feel *very* British, serve with English Roast Potatoes (page 164) and Fred's Applesauce (page 172).

baked ham with mostarda di frutta

Serves 8

FOR THE HAM

One 4- to 4½-pound boneless uncooked ham

2 bay leaves

4 to 6 allspice berries

1 tablespoon whole black peppercorns

2 strips orange peel

1 onion, chopped

1 carrot, chopped

½ tablespoon coriander seeds

6 to 8 whole cloves

FOR THE GLAZE

6 tablespoons soft light brown sugar

2 tablespoons Mostarda di Frutta syrup

1 tablespoon Colman's Mustard Powder

Finely grated zest of ½ orange

Whole cloves, for studding the ham

Light brown sugar, for sprinkling

Fruit from the Mostarda di Frutta syrup, for serving

On certain special occasions my mother would make a succulent baked ham garnished with pineapple and cherries. When it came to doing this book, I wanted to pay homage to her dish but in some way make it our own. So in keeping with this book's cross-cultural culinary theme, this combination of very English Colman's Mustard Powder and very Italian Mostarda di Frutta in the glaze creates our very own Tucci-Blunt ham.

———

Note: You may need to soak the ham before cooking. Refer to your butcher or to manufacturer's instructions.

1. Make the ham: Place the ham, bay leaves, allspice, peppercorns, orange peel, onion, carrot, and coriander in a large, deep saucepan and add just enough water to cover the ham. Bring to a boil over medium heat and cook for 1½ to 2 hours, until the ham's internal temperature registers 180°F on a meat thermometer. As it's cooking, skim off any scum that rises to the surface and make sure you top off the pot with extra boiling water as needed if the ham becomes exposed.

2. Preheat the oven to 425°F. Line a roasting pan with aluminum foil.

3. Gently remove the ham from the water and place it in the prepared pan. When it's cool enough to handle, peel off the skin carefully, keeping the fat intact. Score the fat all over in a diamond pattern.

4. Make the glaze: In a bowl, mix together the glaze ingredients.

5. Brush the glaze all over the ham. Stud the ham with the cloves in the center of the diamonds and bake for 25 to 30 minutes, until golden and bubbling. Baste occasionally, sprinkling on some more sugar as well, if you like.

6. Serve with the fruit from the Mostarda di Frutta on the side.

STANLEY'S TIP

If you like, you can save the ham stock to make a lentil soup or Pea and Ham Hock Soup (page 4).

seared lamb chops

Serves 4 to 6

2 cloves garlic, finely chopped

Leaves from 3 sprigs fresh thyme, chopped

Leaves from 3 sprigs fresh rosemary, chopped

Freshly ground black pepper

¼ cup extra virgin olive oil

12 lamb chops, trimmed

Kosher salt

2 tablespoons olive oil

½ to 1 cup dry white wine

Many years ago I was fortunate enough to dine with the late, great Marcello Mastroianni in Paris. I had met him on the set of the film he was shooting, and having heard me utter a few words of Italian, he invited me to join him and the wonderful producer Jon Kilik for dinner. As Mastroianni was an idol of mine, I was so nervous that I could barely speak. To make matters worse, he spoke little English, and believed me to be fluent in Italian. I *had* indeed learned Italian, while living in Italy when I was twelve, but had not since spoken with any frequency, which I'm sure he realized quite quickly.

However, he never let on and was as charming and gracious as I had always imagined he would be. We ate at his favorite Italian restaurant where, off the menu, he asked for *pasta e fagioli* and these simply prepared lamb chops. The food was truthful, profound, and without affectation, as was Mastroianni himself.

————————

1. In a large bowl, mix together the garlic, thyme, rosemary, pepper, and extra virgin olive oil. Toss the lamb through the mixture and set aside to marinate for at least 20 minutes, preferably an hour.

2. In a large sauté pan, heat olive oil over medium-high heat. Fry the chops for 3 to 5 minutes on each side until cooked to your liking. Pressing the flesh in the center of each chop will allow you to gauge its level of doneness. The firmer the meat, the more done it is.

3. Set them aside and add the garlic and rosemary from the marinade to the pan. Cook until the garlic takes color, then deglaze the pan with ½ to 1 cup wine and cook, stirring in any juices from the lamb, until reduced into a sauce.

Alternatively, while the lamb chops are marinating, heat your broiler to high.

4. Scrape off the excess marinade from the chops, place them in an enamel roasting pan and season them generously with salt. Place them under the broiler for 3 to 5 minutes on each side, until done to your liking. Follow the steps above to make the sauce.

STANLEY'S TIP

Note that you want your lamb chops well trimmed so that the rib bone can act as a handle.

shepherd's pie

This was a Blunt family favorite when Felicity was growing up. She says, "Mum would ask us what we wanted for dinner, and shepherd's pie was always my answer. (My sister's was pasta Bolognese.) When I moved to the US, this became a favorite British import. If you can only find ground beef, that's fine—though technically that changes the recipe to cottage pie.

"I often make two of these at a time, then freeze one for later. I make the mashed potatoes with olive oil, as a few family members are lactose intolerant, but if you want a richer mash, do substitute butter and milk."

———

1. Make the filling: In a large, heavy-bottomed saucepan, heat 2 tablespoons of the olive oil over medium heat. Add the onions, garlic, carrots, and celery and cook until the vegetables have softened, 5 to 8 minutes. Remove from the pan and set aside.

2. Heat the remaining 1 tablespoon olive oil in the pan. When it is nice and hot, add the ground lamb and anchovies and cook until the meat has browned. You will probably need to do this in batches. If water comes out of the meat, keep pouring it off as it appears; otherwise, your meat will boil and start to become rubbery.

3. While the meat is browning, place the cooked vegetables in a food processor and pulse so they are uniformly small.

4. Once the meat has browned, reduce the heat and return the vegetables to the pan. Add the thyme and rosemary.

5. Add the red wine and cook until the liquid has reduced by half. Add the chopped tomatoes and cook for 2 minutes more. Add the chicken stock and stir through the meat. Season with salt and

Serves 6 to 8

FOR THE FILLING

3 tablespoons olive oil

2 medium red onions, coarsely chopped

4 cloves garlic, sliced

4 carrots, peeled and chopped

3 celery stalks, coarsely chopped

2 pounds good quality ground lamb

3 anchovies

Leaves from 2 sprigs fresh thyme, chopped

Leaves from 1 sprig fresh rosemary, chopped

1 cup red wine

One 14-ounce can chopped tomatoes

1½ cups chicken stock

Kosher salt and freshly ground black pepper

FOR THE MASHED POTATOES

2 pounds floury potatoes, peeled and cut into 1- to 2-inch chunks

Kosher salt and freshly ground black pepper

½ to 1 cup extra virgin olive oil

2 to 4 tablespoons (¼ to ½ stick) butter (optional)

recipe continued on next page

pepper. Cook, stirring occasionally, for about 20 minutes. Cover the pan, leaving the lid slightly ajar, reduce the heat to low, and cook for 20 minutes more.

6. Taste the meat. If it hasn't softened sufficiently, add a half cup of chicken stock and cook, with the lid ajar, for 20 minutes more.

7. Make the mashed potatoes: Place the potatoes in a large saucepan with a pinch of salt and add enough water to cover. Bring the water to a boil and cook until the potatoes are cooked through, approximately 15 minutes. Drain and return the potatoes to the saucepan, setting them aside with the lid on for a few minutes to help them soften further. Mash them well, season with salt and pepper, then add the olive oil, mashing until silky smooth and adding more oil as needed. If you like, you can also add the butter for extra richness.

8. Assemble the pie: Preheat the oven to 400°F.

9. Spread the meat over the bottom of a baking dish. Spoon the mashed potatoes in healthy spoonfuls over the top and spread evenly. Then take a fork and run it across the top to create little rivulets. Drizzle with some olive oil and bake for 35 to 40 minutes, until the top is golden brown.

STANLEY'S TIP

Serve with peas on the side.

pan-seared loin of venison with red wine, juniper, and quince

Serves 2

FOR THE MARINADE

1 cup red wine

1 tablespoon juniper berries, lightly crushed

2 bay leaves

A few whole black or green peppercorns, lightly crushed

FOR THE VENISON

One 8- to 10-ounce loin of venison

1 tablespoon olive oil

Kosher salt and freshly ground black pepper

1 tablespoon quince jelly

Leaves from 1 sprig fresh thyme

1 tablespoon unsalted butter, cold

Deer are so plentiful in the United States, but people are still wary of eating venison. If you are one of those people, you can substitute beef tenderloin here, but I would argue that venison has a richer, deeper flavor, not to mention being much leaner.

———————

1. Make the marinade: In a large bowl, combine the marinade ingredients and mix well.

2. Make the venison: Place the venison in the marinade and set aside to marinate for 1 to 3 hours.

3. Remove the venison from the marinade and pat dry. Reserve the marinade.

4. In a heavy pan, heat the olive oil until very hot. Season the venison with salt and pepper and sear it in the pan for 3 to 5 minutes per side for rare to medium-rare, depending on the thickness of the loin. Remove the venison from the pan and set aside to rest on a warm plate for at least 5 minutes. Strain the marinade through a sieve into the pan and bring to a boil, until it is bubbling furiously. Stir in the quince jelly and the thyme and cook until the marinade has reduced by half. Stir in the cold butter at the end to enrich the sauce and give it a little gloss.

5. Slice the venison on an angle and serve with the sauce.

• In the UK, they often use red currant jelly instead of quince jelly. Feel free to make the substitution if you can find some.

• If you plan to use beef tenderloin instead of venison, make sure you only marinate it for a half hour or so—it doesn't need more.

• It goes without saying that every piece of meat you cook is different, so the timing will always vary. The best way to check if it's done, be it a piece of venison like this or a steak, is by pressing it gently but firmly with your finger. The less resistance it gives you, the rarer it is; the more resistance, the more well done.

rabbit with cipollini onions and tomato

Rabbit is quite prevalent on the Italian table. I grew up eating it because my grandparents raised a few, but prior to the Second World War, it was eaten throughout most of America. Today, it has all but disappeared from the American table, which is unfortunate, as it is a plentiful, sustainable, delicious, lean meat.

If you are lucky enough to get a rabbit with its liver, be sure to set the liver aside and follow the recipe on the following page.

———————

1. Preheat the oven to 375°F. Position a rack in the middle of the oven.

2. In a Dutch oven, heat the olive oil over medium-high heat. Add the pancetta and cook for 2 to 3 minutes, until golden and crispy. Add the salami, reduce the heat to medium, and continue to cook for 2 minutes more. Add the fennel seeds and garlic, stirring continuously, and cook until the garlic has softened. Remove the ingredients from pan and set aside.

3. Season the rabbit pieces well with salt and pepper. Add a little more oil to the pan, if needed, and brown the rabbit pieces. You may need to do this in batches so that you don't overcrowd the pan. Be careful not to burn the rabbit—it is very lean. When it's nicely colored, return everything to the pan and add the wine, stock, onions, tomatoes, and thyme. Be sure to coat the rabbit with the liquid. Add a pinch of salt and pepper and simmer for a minute. Then add a drizzle of extra virgin olive oil, cover, and bake for 40 minutes.

4. Remove from the oven, take out the rabbit pieces, and set them aside. Set the Dutch oven on the stove top over low to medium heat and cook until the liquid in the pan has reduced to a thickened, silky sauce, 8 to 12 minutes.

5. Return the rabbit pieces to the pan and heat through before serving. Finish with some freshly chopped fennel fronds and serve immediately.

Serves 2 to 4

2 tablespoons olive oil

¼ cup pancetta, finely diced

1 tablespoon Genoa salami, finely diced

½ teaspoon fennel seeds

2 cloves garlic, minced

1 whole rabbit, jointed

Kosher salt and freshly ground black pepper

½ cup dry white wine

2 cups chicken stock

6 to 8 small white cipollini onions, halved

4 Campari or medium tomatoes, halved

3 sprigs fresh thyme

Extra virgin olive oil

1 tablespoon finely chopped fennel fronds, to finish

sauteéd rabbit liver

Serves 2

1 rabbit liver

1 cup milk

Kosher salt and freshly
ground black pepper

1½ tablespoons butter

2 tablespoons dry
vermouth, such as Dolin
or Noilly Prat

Pinch of chopped fresh
flat-leaf parsley

½ teaspoon kosher salt

Squeeze of fresh lemon
juice

Toasted bread, for
serving

If you are lucky enough to get the liver along with your rabbit, don't let it go to waste; try this recipe.

———————

1. In a bowl, place the liver in the milk and let it soak for 20 minutes.

2. Remove the liver and pat dry. Season with salt and pepper.

3. In a sauté pan, heat the butter over medium-high heat until almost brown. Raise the heat to high and place the liver in the sauté pan; toss for 1 minute. Add the vermouth and parsley and cook, tossing continuously, for 1 to 2 minutes more.

4. Remove from the heat and add salt and pepper to taste and a squeeze of fresh lemon.

5. Serve with the toasted bread.

roast chicken

Serves 4 to 6

6 tablespoons butter

1 shallot, finely chopped

1 clove garlic, finely chopped

Leaves from 2 sprigs fresh rosemary

Leaves from 4 sprigs fresh thyme

5 to 6 fresh sage leaves

One 3-pound chicken

Kosher salt and freshly ground black pepper

½ lemon

½ onion

½ cup water or white wine

Everyone loves a roast chicken. It makes the whole house smell good, and it's at the apex of comfort foods. Using the carcass to make stock (page 208) or soup is an added benefit.

———————

1. Preheat the oven to 350°F.

2. In a small frying pan, heat 4 tablespoons of the butter over low heat. Add the shallot and garlic along with the chopped leaves of 1 sprig rosemary, 2 sprigs thyme, and 2 sage leaves and cook until the shallot and garlic are soft. Set aside to cool.

3. Gently lift the skin from the chicken breast to create a pocket. Slip a small paring knife inside and cut anything that connects the skin to the breast, without piercing the skin. Using your fingers or a spoon, work the cooled herb mixture into the pocket under the skin of the chicken. Season the cavity with salt and pepper, and insert the lemon, onion, and the remaining herbs into the cavity. Slather the bird's skin with the remaining 2 tablespoons of butter, season with salt, and place the chicken on a rack set in a roasting pan. Pour the water or white wine into the pan.

4. Roast for 1½ to 2 hours, basting every 20 minutes or so. If you feel that the skin is turning too dark at any point, cover the breast with a piece of aluminum foil for the remainder of the cooking time. Test for doneness—if you stab the chicken's thigh with a skewer, the juices will run clear—and set aside to rest for 15 minutes before carving.

cornish game hens
with sage and pancetta

Serves 4

4 Cornish game hens

Kosher salt and freshly
ground black pepper

2 shallots, halved

4 cloves garlic

8 fresh sage leaves

2 tablespoons butter

2 tablespoons olive oil

12 to 16 slices pancetta
or bacon

1 cup white wine

These diminutive birds are a great alternative to roast chicken. They take very little time to cook, and the option of serving one per person makes the meal seem quite special.

———————

1. Preheat the oven to 400°F.

2. Season the cavities of the Cornish game hens with salt and pepper and insert half a shallot, a garlic clove, and a sage leaf into each. Place ½ tablespoon of the butter in the cavity of each bird as well. Rub the birds with the olive oil and season the breasts with salt and pepper. Place a sage leaf on the back of each bird and drape each with 3 or 4 slices of the pancetta.

3. Roast for 45 to 50 minutes. Halfway through roasting, remove the pancetta from the breasts of the birds and place it beside them. Baste the birds with the roasting juices and continue to cook for the remaining time. To check if they are cooked, stab the birds in the thickest part of the thigh with a skewer. If the juice runs clear, then they are done.

4. Remove the birds from the oven, together with the pancetta, and place them on a warm plate to rest. Set the roasting pan on the stove top over medium heat. When the juices in the pan begin to bubble, pour in the wine. Deglaze the pan, scraping up any residue, and cook until the liquid has reduced by half.

5. Serve with Polenta Frites (page 159) and the reduced pan *jus* on the side.

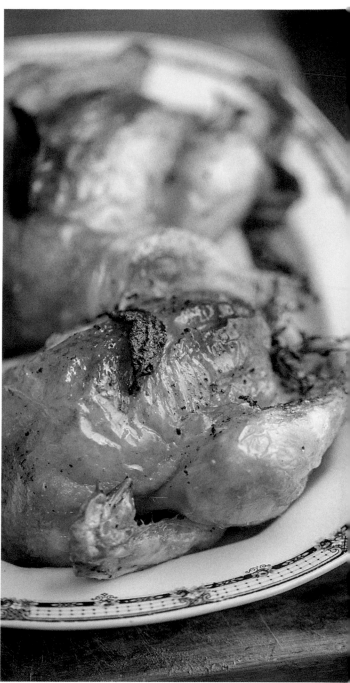

chicken wings with homemade barbecue sauce

Serves 4 to 6

1 cup soy sauce

½ cup ketchup

¼ cup honey

2 pounds chicken wings

This is another one of Kate's recipes. Again, she never wrote it down, so it has been a case of trial and error and many nostalgic tastings to get to this interpretation. These wings are sticky and sweet and seem to disappear very quickly when kids are around.

———————

1. In a large bowl, whisk together the soy sauce, ketchup, and honey. Add the chicken wings and set aside to marinate for an hour or two at room temperature.

2. Preheat the oven to 400°F. Line a baking sheet with aluminum foil.

3. Place the wings on the prepared baking sheet, reserving the marinade, and bake for 30 to 35 minutes, basting at the halfway stage, until crisp and burnished.

joan's chicken wings

My mom makes these crisp, golden wings with a hint of garlic and herbs. Joan says: "These are so simple to make and just by adding some vegetables you turn them into a complete meal."

———————

1. Preheat the oven to 375°F.

2. Trim the tips off the wings and set the tips aside to use in Chicken Stock (page 208). Cut the wing joints into two pieces. Place the wings in a large baking dish and coat them well in 3 tablespoons of the olive oil. Add the rosemary, sage, and oregano. Season with salt and pepper.

3. In a bowl, toss the potato, carrots, and scallion with the remaining 1 tablespoon oil. Season with a little salt and pepper. Add these to the baking dish with the wings and mix well.

4. Bake for 15 minutes, then add the wine and bake for 15 minutes more. At this point, if the wings look like they are not browning, raise the oven temperature to 400°F. Add the tomatoes and give it all a good toss so the chicken gets crisped on all sides. Return to the oven for 10 minutes more, until everything is cooked through. The chicken should be golden, and the tomatoes should be soft and melting. Stir in the parsley and serve.

JOAN'S TIPS

• These are even good cold.

• You can freeze the wing tips to use in stock at a later date.

Serves 6

2 pounds chicken wings

4 tablespoons olive oil

2 large sprigs fresh rosemary, broken up

3 fresh sage leaves

Good pinch of dried wild oregano

Kosher salt and freshly ground black pepper

1 large Yukon Gold potato, peeled and cut into chunks

2 large carrots, peeled and sliced

1 large scallion, sliced

¼ cup dry white wine

4 to 6 Campari tomatoes

1 tablespoon chopped fresh flat-leaf parsley

sides

"One of the first times we cooked together, Felicity suggested making roast potatoes. I said, 'Sure,' thinking she meant potatoes cut up and thrown in the oven with some olive oil. It was then that she began a process the likes of which I had never seen. First, she parboiled the potatoes. Then she 'fluffed' them by violently shaking them in a lidded pot like a madwoman. She then proceeded to heat a copious amount of oil, or the fat from an entire gaggle of geese, to almost volcanic temperatures for what she described as the 'final phase.' It was then that my parents, the children, and I slowly crept out of the kitchen, convinced she was going to burn down the house and us along with it. But one bite of those extraordinary spuds, and we were willing to risk immolation any day of the week."

—Stanley

asparagus with lemon butter

Serves 4

1 pound asparagus
spears, trimmed

4 tablespoons butter

½ teaspoon lemon zest

1 tablespoon freshly
squeezed lemon juice

Kosher salt and freshly
ground black pepper

These spears of al dente asparagus dripping with sharp, lemony butter can accompany meat, fish, or fowl. You can even serve these as a starter.

———————

1. Bring a saucepan of salted water to a boil. Cook the asparagus for 2½ to 3 minutes, then drain and transfer to a serving platter.

2. In a frying pan, gently melt the butter over low heat. Stir in the lemon zest and juice. Season with salt and pepper.

3. Serve the asparagus with the lemon butter drizzled on top.

mashed potatoes

Serves 4 to 6

2 pounds russet potatoes, peeled and cut into 1- to 2-inch chunks

½ to 1 cup extra virgin olive oil

Kosher salt and freshly ground black pepper

2 to 4 tablespoons (¼ to ½ stick) butter

1 egg yolk (optional)

Mashed potatoes are one of the supreme comfort foods. Felicity came up with this version made with olive oil because I can't have cream or milk, but thankfully a little butter is fine. The egg yolk adds extra richness at the end.

Find the flouriest potatoes you can—russets are a good choice. Waxy potatoes mean a mash that is heavy rather than light.

———————

Place the potatoes in a large saucepan with a pinch of salt and add enough water to cover. Bring the water to a boil and cook the potatoes until they are soft. Drain and return them to the hot pan. Set aside for a couple of minutes to let the last of the water evaporate. The steam will finish them off and help you avoid any lumps. Then mash the potatoes with the olive oil, and season with salt and pepper to taste. How much olive oil you need will depend on your potatoes' absorbency. Finally, beat in the butter with a fork, followed by, if you're feeling really indulgent, the egg yolk.

tangled greens

These dark, almost bitter greens sautéed with garlic and chiles complement red meat perfectly.

———————

1. Wash the greens in a colander and set aside.

2. In a large sauté pan, heat the olive oil over medium heat. Add the garlic and the peperoncini (if using) and cook until the garlic is just beginning to color. Remove the peperoncini and set aside, then add the greens with any residual water that clings to them. Season with salt and cook, stirring often, until the greens are just wilted but still retain some texture. Drizzle with a little extra virgin olive oil and serve immediately.

Serves 4 to 6

1 pound greens, such as black kale or chard, trimmed and chopped, tough lower part of the stems removed

2 tablespoons olive oil

2 to 4 cloves garlic, sliced

2 to 3 peperoncini (optional)

Kosher salt

Extra virgin olive oil, for drizzling

grilled spring onions

Serves 4 to 6

12 to 16 large spring onions, halved lengthwise

1 tablespoon olive oil

Good pinch of kosher salt

Extra virgin olive oil, for drizzling

When we were living in Westchester, we would buy these fresh, fat, spring onions. We'd split them in half, toss them in extra virgin olive oil and salt, and throw them on the grill. The smell alone is tantalizing—charred, pungent perfection.

————————

1. In a bowl, toss the spring onions with the olive oil and season them with the salt. Then toss them again.

2. Preheat a grill to medium-high, or heat a ridged griddle over medium-high heat. Cook the onions for 3 to 5 minutes, turning once or twice, until the greens have wilted and they have good, deep char marks on them.

3. Place the onions on a warm plate, drizzle with extra virgin olive oil, and serve immediately.

STANLEY'S TIP

If you have any of these left over (though God knows why you would, they're so delicious), they make a great addition to a Frittata (page 31).

fried green tomatoes

I fell in love with green tomatoes prepared this way in a restaurant in Atlanta while shooting *The Hunger Games*.

These are great with Basic Mayonnaise (page 218).

—————

1. Season the tomatoes on both sides with salt and pepper and set aside for 20 minutes or so. Transfer the tomatoes to paper towels to dry.

2. Beat the egg in a small bowl. Place the flour in a second bowl and the cornmeal in a third. Season the flour and cornmeal with salt and pepper.

3. In a large frying pan, heat ¼ cup of the oil over medium-high heat. Dip each piece of tomato lightly into the flour first, then the egg, and then the cornmeal, shaking off any excess as you go, and fry them in batches for about 3 minutes on each side, until golden brown. You may need to add the remaining oil as you go. Set the fried tomatoes aside on paper towels to drain, and serve.

Serves 4

4 to 6 green tomatoes, cut into ½-inch slices

Kosher salt and freshly ground black pepper

1 large egg

¼ cup all-purpose flour

1 cup cornmeal

½ cup vegetable oil or bacon fat

lentils

Serves 6

2 tablespoons olive oil

1 large onion, finely chopped

1 shallot, finely chopped

1 carrot, finely chopped

1 celery stalk, finely chopped

2 cloves garlic, finely chopped

3 cups Puy lentils, rinsed

Water or chicken stock

1 bay leaf

Good pinch of ground cumin

Good pinch of freshly ground white pepper

Kosher salt and freshly ground black pepper

Grated lemon zest

Handful of fresh flat-leaf parsley, chopped

Extra virgin olive oil, for drizzling

Lentils aren't just a delicious side dish—they're also a simple, complete meal when served with rice, pasta, or couscous. I often make a large batch and store them in the fridge to eat throughout the week.

————————

1. In a heavy-bottomed saucepan, heat the olive oil over medium heat. Add the onion, shallot, carrot, celery, and garlic, and gently cook until soft without letting the mixture color, 7 to 10 minutes. Add the lentils and stir to coat well with the oil. Add enough water or chicken stock to cover them generously and add the bay leaf, cumin, and white pepper. Season with salt and black pepper. Bring to a boil, then reduce the heat to low, partially covering the pan with a lid. Simmer until the lentils are cooked, 20 to 25 minutes, adding more water or stock if the lentils look too dry.

2. Once the lentils have cooked, taste and adjust the seasoning. Add the lemon zest and parsley and finish with a good drizzle of extra virgin olive oil.

baked beans

This is another one of Kate's recipes we have re-created. The kids love it served with Chicken Wings with Homemade Barbecue Sauce (page 140). Because this is so good, I've never even attempted to make baked beans from scratch.

———————

1. Preheat the oven to 325°F.

2. In a heavy-bottomed pan, heat the oil over low to medium heat. Add the onion and sauté until just softened. Remove the onion from the pan and set aside to cool a bit. Place the onion in a medium bowl with the mustard, ketchup, molasses, and sugar and mix well.

3. Pour the baked beans into a baking dish along with the onion mixture and stir together well. Lay the bacon over the beans and bake for 45 minutes, until the beans have turned a darker color and have reduced a bit.

Serves 4 to 6

1 tablespoon vegetable oil

¼ onion, finely minced

2 tablespoons prepared yellow mustard

2 tablespoons ketchup

2 tablespoons molasses

2 teaspoons brown sugar

One 32-ounce can Bush's baked beans

3 to 4 fat slices bacon

sautéed mushrooms

This is a very versatile dish. Mushrooms prepared this way work as a side dish but can also be incorporated into a number of other dishes, including pasta, risotto, and polenta.

———

1. In a heavy-bottomed sauté pan, heat 3 tablespoons of the olive oil over a low heat. Add the garlic and fry gently until fragrant but not brown—you want only to infuse the oil with the garlic flavor. Remove the garlic from the pan with a slotted spoon and discard.

2. Raise the heat to medium and, after a few seconds, add the chestnut mushrooms. You may need to add a little more oil at this stage. Toss to coat with the fragrant oil until they begin to color, 3 to 5 minutes.

3. Add the chanterelles and the butter. Turn them and toss for another minute or so. Season with salt and pepper and stir in the parsley. Serve immediately.

STANLEY'S TIP

These are also delicious as part of an antipasto platter or as a light lunch, served with some goat cheese and fresh bread.

Serves 4 to 6, as a side

3 to 4 tablespoons extra virgin olive oil

1 clove garlic, finely slivered

7 ounces chestnut mushrooms, trimmed and sliced

7 ounces chanterelle mushrooms, cleaned

1 tablespoon butter

Sea salt and freshly ground black pepper

Small handful of fresh flat-leaf parsley, finely chopped

polenta

Serves 4 to 6

3 cups water

1 cup milk (optional)

2½ teaspoons salt

2 tablespoons olive oil

1¼ cups polenta

2 tablespoons butter

2 tablespoons freshly
grated Parmigiano-
Reggiano

Kosher salt and freshly
ground black pepper

Extra virgin olive oil, for
drizzling

All brands of polenta behave differently, so use this recipe as a blueprint. Choose your favorite type—be it coarse or fine, hand-milled or quick-cook—check the instructions on the package, and then make the recipe your own.

If you don't want to use the milk in this recipe, make sure you replace it with the same volume of water.

———————

1. In a medium saucepan, bring the water and milk (if using) to a boil over medium-high heat. Add the salt and olive oil and reduce the heat to low. Add the polenta and simmer, stirring, for about 30 minutes until the polenta has cooked. It should be thick, tender, and pourable. Stir in the butter and Parmigiano and season to taste with salt and freshly ground pepper.

2. Either serve immediately, topped with a drizzle of extra virgin olive oil, with the Sautéed Mushrooms (page 155) or the Pan-Seared Loin of Venison (page 128), or pour it into a 9 x 13-inch baking pan to cool. You can use this to make Polenta Frites (page 159), or cut it into slices to pan-fry or grill.

polenta frites

These are a great alternative to French fries, especially when you have some leftover polenta. Served sprinkled with some coarse kosher salt and chopped rosemary, they are a delicious side or *cicchetti* to serve with wine.

———————

1. The day before you want to serve these, make a batch of Polenta (page 156). Pour it into a greased baking tray, then set aside to cool. Cover and refrigerate until needed.

2. Remove the polenta gently from the pan and cut it into 2½ x ½ x ½-inch chunks—think of a chunky French fry. Then gently roll each one in the Parmigiano. Place the polenta frites on a sheet of parchment paper on a baking sheet, then put them in the fridge until needed.

3. When you're ready to cook, heat the oil in a deep fryer to 350°F. Working in batches, fry the polenta frites until crisp and golden, 3 to 4 minutes per batch. Using the basket, remove the frites and set aside to drain on paper towels. While still hot, season with salt and fresh rosemary and serve immediately.

4. Alternatively, heat ¼ inch vegetable oil in a heavy cast-iron sauté pan. You don't want the oil to cover the polenta frites, you want it just to bubble to the top of the frites when they are added. When the oil is hot enough (i.e., when it cooks a piece of bread to golden) place a few frites at a time into the hot oil (being careful not to overcrowd the pan), turning them every now and then until they are crisp and golden on all sides—about 5 minutes. Remove the polenta frites with a slotted spoon and set aside to drain on paper towels before seasoning with salt, fresh rosemary, and some extra Parmigiano.

Serves 4 to 6

Cooked Polenta, cold; see quantities (page 156)

¼ to ½ cup freshly grated Parmigiano-Reggiano

Vegetable oil, for deep-frying

Kosher salt

Leaves from 2 sprigs fresh rosemary, chopped

vegetable parmigiana

Serves 4 to 6

1 large eggplant, halved lengthwise, then cut lengthwise at an angle into long, ¼-inch-thick slices

2 large potatoes, peeled, halved lengthwise, and cut into half-moons (optional)

3 zucchini, cut lengthwise into thin strips

2 large tomatoes, halved and cut into half-moons

5 to 7 tablespoons olive oil (about ½ cup)

Kosher salt and freshly ground black pepper

½ cup bread crumbs

2 tablespoons fresh thyme, finely chopped

2 tablespoons fresh oregano, finely chopped

½ cup freshly grated Parmigiano-Reggiano

1 to 2 cloves garlic, finely chopped

This is a combination of my mother's eggplant Parmigiana and a French *tian*. With the addition of the potato, this makes a great vegetarian main course or a single side dish that combines a starch and a vegetable.

———————

1. Preheat the broiler to medium-high.

2. Spread the eggplant, potato (if using), and zucchini slices on individual baking sheets, one for each ingredient, coat with 2 tablespoons of the olive oil, and season with salt. Then place them under the broiler until they start to color, 3 to 5 minutes. This will evaporate some of their water so that they don't go soggy in the final dish.

3. Preheat the oven to 350°F.

4. Combine the bread crumbs, half of the chopped herbs, half of the grated cheese, and a dash of salt and pepper in a bowl and set aside.

5. Combine the remaining herb mixture, grated cheese, all of the garlic, and a dash of salt and pepper in another bowl.

6. Coat the bottom and sides of a rectangular baking dish with 2 tablespoons of the olive oil.

7. From one short side of the dish, stack the eggplant, zucchini, potato (if using), and tomatoes so that they stand upright on edge against one another. Sprinkle a little of the chopped herb, garlic, and cheese mixture in between some of the layers as you work your way across the baking dish.

8. When completed, drizzle the remaining olive oil over the top and sprinkle with the bread-crumb mixture.

9. Bake for 30 to 40 minutes. Check it just before the end of the baking time. If it looks a little dry, drizzle with a little extra olive oil. Serve warm or at room temperature, not hot.

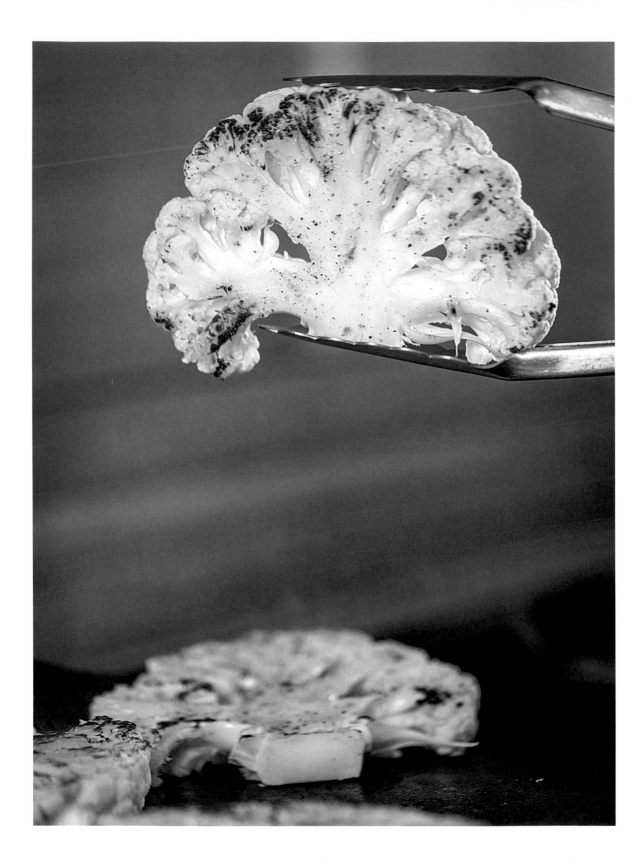

roasted cauliflower steaks

"Cauliflower was something I abhorred growing up," says Felicity. "It was always served in cheese or milk sauces to disguise its sometimes potent taste. Recently I had it in thick, steak-like, oven-roasted slices, and I was completely won over. These are also great as a starter or on their own or with a salad or tart yogurt."

————————

1. Preheat the oven to 400°F.

2. Trim the leaves and the protruding part of the stem from the cauliflower. Carefully cut the head into thick slices, about ¾-inch wide. (The fresher your cauliflower, the easier it will be to retain whole slices.)

3. Brush the "steaks" with olive oil on both sides, then season each side with salt and pepper and the cumin.

4. Heat a cast-iron pan over high heat. Working with one piece at a time, sear the cauliflower on each side for a minute, turning carefully, until golden.

5. Place the seared cauliflower steaks on a baking sheet and bake for 15 to 20 minutes, until soft.

Serves 6

1 head cauliflower

Olive oil, for brushing

Kosher salt and freshly ground black pepper

1 teaspoon ground cumin

english roast potatoes

Serves 4

2 pounds russet potatoes, peeled and cut into 2-inch pieces

2 to 3 tablespoons vegetable oil

Kosher salt

This was Felicity's grandmother's method. By parboiling the potatoes first and then roasting them in incredibly hot oil, you end up with a wonderful crunchy outside and a fluffy, soft inside. The most important thing is to make a real effort to fluff up the outsides before the potatoes go into the very hot oil. These go perfectly with roasted meat.

———

1. Preheat the oven to 400°F.

2. Place the potatoes in a large saucepan with a pinch of salt and add enough water to cover. Bring the water to a boil and parboil the potatoes for about 10 minutes. (Do not overcook them—otherwise you will end up with mush at the next step. The outsides need to be just soft enough to be scored with a fork.) Drain the potatoes and return them to the pan. Put the lid on the pan and shake the hell out of it, breaking up and fluffing the outsides of the potato pieces. Set aside.

3. Pour the oil into a roasting pan and place it in the oven until it's *really* hot. When it's hot, remove the pan from the oven and place it on the stove top over low heat. Put the potatoes in the oil and turn them in it several times. Then roast them in the oven for a good hour, turning them twice during the cooking time.

———

FELICITY'S TIP

Substitute duck or goose fat, if you can get it, for the vegetable oil. It makes a profound difference—the quintessential English roast potato!

roasted root vegetables with thyme

Beets and carrots are two humble root vegetables that take on unctuous depth and sweetness when slow-roasted. If you can find heirloom carrots in rainbow hues and a mixture of red and gold beets, this makes for a beautifully colorful plate designed to stimulate even the most jaded winter appetite.

—————

1. Preheat the oven to 375°F.

2. On a baking sheet, toss the vegetables and the thyme with olive oil and season with salt and pepper.

3. Bake for 30 to 40 minutes, until the vegetables have softened and started to caramelize at the edges. Scatter the seeds over the vegetables and return to the oven for 5 to 10 minutes more.

4. Serve hot or at room temperature.

Serves 4 to 6

8 carrots, peeled and quartered lengthwise

3 to 4 beets, peeled and quartered

6 to 8 sprigs fresh thyme

Extra virgin olive oil

Kosher salt and freshly ground black pepper

2 tablespoons hulled, salted sunflower seeds

2 tablespoons hulled, salted pumpkin seeds

yorkshire pudding

**Makes 18 small
Yorkshire puddings**

2 cups all-purpose flour

1 teaspoon kosher salt

4 medium eggs, beaten

2½ cups 2% milk

3 tablespoons vegetable
oil

These are a light and fluffy side dish similar to popovers that are traditionally served with roast beef. They can be made as individual portions or you can also heat oil in a deep baking dish and make one big one to cut it into slices. Most kids love the individual ones as they can fill them with gravy.

———————

1. Place the flour and salt in a bowl. Create a well and pour in the beaten eggs, whisking as you go and pulling flour in from the sides to create a smooth paste. Once you've added all of the egg, start adding the milk while continuing to whisk and pull all of the flour into the mix. Beat until smooth. Place in the fridge for at least 30 minutes.

2. Preheat the oven to 425°F. Place a small amount of vegetable oil in each well of a muffin tray. Place the tray in the oven and allow the oil to get extremely hot (about 15 minutes).

3. Remove the batter from the fridge and the hot tray from the oven. Drop a ladleful of the batter into each well, filling them to just below the brim. The batter should sizzle as you do this; if not, the oil is not hot enough. Put the tray back into the oven quickly. Close the door and do not open it for 15 minutes. Check at the 15-minute mark and cook for another 5 minutes if the puddings are not golden brown. The Yorkshire puddings will rise up high in their trays and should pop out easily. Eat them straight away.

roasted tomatoes

Serves 4

8 to 12 Campari or
cherry tomatoes, halved

2 tablespoons extra
virgin olive oil

Kosher salt and freshly
ground black pepper

Felicity is addicted to these. Luckily, they are very easy to make. Slow-roasted in the oven until they collapse and become soft and jammy, they should be served immediately as a side or to complement a pasta or rice dish. If you won't be using them immediately, store them in the fridge covered with a thin layer of good olive oil.

———————

1. Preheat the oven to 250°F.

2. Place the tomatoes on a baking sheet, cut-side up. Drizzle them with the olive oil, season them with salt and pepper, and bake them in the oven for at least an hour and a half—the longer, the better.

STANLEY'S TIP

These will keep fully submerged in a jar of olive oil in the refrigerator for about 1 week.

fred's applesauce

Serves 6

3 to 4 Granny Smith apples, peeled, cored, and sliced

Juice of ½ lemon

1 tablespoon brown sugar

1 tablespoon superfine sugar

1 sprig fresh rosemary

½ ounce butter

"When we were growing up, there was an apple tree in my garden," says Felicity. "And when they were in season, the whole yard was a carpet of windfall apples. We would collect them and Mum would spend the weekend making applesauce. It was so delicious that we would eat bowls of it. This recipe comes from our friend Fred and has a hint of rosemary, just to add some depth. In England, it would be made with Bramley apples. They are very tart, and they cook very well. Some people say that Northern Spy apples make a good substitute, but here I'm using Granny Smiths."

As you're peeling, coring, and slicing the apples, toss the pieces in the lemon juice to keep them from discoloring. Then place all the ingredients in a small saucepan with a splash of water and cook gently over medium-low heat until the apples break down into a sauce. Serve hot or cold with the Roasted Pork Belly (pages 116–17).

onion rings

Sweet on the inside, crispy and crunchy on the outside, these onion rings are addictive. Unfortunately, they are also very easy to make.

———————

1. Sift the flour into a bowl with the baking powder and salt. Add the onion rings and toss to thoroughly coat. Remove the onion rings and set aside.

2. Add the egg and milk to the remaining flour mixture and mix thoroughly until there are no lumps. If you think the batter looks a little thin at this point, add another ¼ cup flour. Place the bread crumbs in a shallow bowl.

3. Dredge the floured onion rings through the batter and set aside on a rack so that the excess drips off. It's a good idea to place the rack over some parchment paper—to help you clean up! Once the excess batter has dripped off the onion rings, dredge them through the bread crumbs until they are well coated and set aside.

4. Heat the vegetable oil to 350°F in a deep-fryer. Working in batches, fry the onion rings until golden. Alternatively, heat 2 inches of oil in a heavy, high-sided saucepan over medium-high heat until it registers 350°F on a deep-fry thermometer, and, again, cook the onion rings in batches. If you choose to cook them this way, take extra care as the fat can "spit," and you can easily get burned.

5. Remove the onion rings with tongs and set aside on paper towels to drain. Serve hot.

Serves 2 to 4

1¼ cups all-purpose flour, plus more as needed

1 teaspoon baking powder

2 teaspoons kosher salt

1 large or 2 medium white onions, cut into ¼-inch-thick rings

1 large egg

1 cup milk

1 to 1½ cups bread crumbs (the drier the better)

Vegetable oil, for deep-frying

desserts

"Neither Felicity nor I have an especially sweet tooth. Even when it came to our wedding cake, we asked that it be made out of wheels of cheese. However, the dessert recipes here are some of our favorites."

—Stanley

blueberry pie

"One of my first holidays with Stanley and the kids as a family was in Martha's Vineyard, where blueberry pie was an obligatory end to each meal," says Felicity. "We would race from the beach back to the house to see who could get to the previous night's leftover pie first. Isabel always won! I knew that if I was going to be marrying into an American family, I had to learn the art of the blueberry pie.

"I prefer a very short and buttery pastry, so it may be a little soft when rolling out, but it is flaky and delicious when cooked."

---

1. Make the pastry: Put the flour in a large bowl. Cut the butter into small pieces, add it to the flour, and rub it in using your fingertips until you have a bread-crumb–like texture. Stir in the sugar and salt. Add ice water 1 teaspoon at a time until the pastry comes together. Form it into a ball and wrap it in plastic wrap. Put it in the fridge for 30 minutes to chill.

2. Make the filling: In a large bowl, mix together all the filling ingredients with your hands.

3. Assemble the pie: Preheat the oven to 350°F. Butter a 9-inch pie dish.

4. Divide the pastry dough in two, making one piece a bit bigger than the other, as the larger piece will be your base. Roll out the pastry for the base until it's wide enough to overhang the pie dish by a half inch. Lay it into the dish and put in the filling. Roll out the second piece of pastry, place it over the top, and crimp the two pastry sections together. Place the pie in the fridge for 20 minutes to rest.

Serves 6 to 8

FOR THE PASTRY

2¼ cups all-purpose flour

16 tablespoons (2 sticks) butter, chilled

2 tablespoons superfine sugar

Pinch of kosher salt

Ice water

FOR THE FILLING

8 cups fresh blueberries

½ teaspoon lemon zest

1 tablespoon freshly squeezed lemon juice

¼ cup all-purpose flour

½ cup superfine sugar

¼ teaspoon ground cinnamon

2 tablespoons butter, cut into small pieces

TO ASSEMBLE

Butter, for the pan

1 egg, beaten

1 tablespoon milk

2 tablespoons superfine sugar

recipe continued on next page

5. When you're ready to bake, remove the pie from the fridge. Mix the egg and milk together in a small bowl and brush a light coating of this egg wash over the top of the pastry. Make four small cuts in the top crust so the steam can escape, and dust it with the sugar.

6. Bake the pie for 40 minutes, until the crust is golden brown. Remove and let cool for a bit. Serve with cream or ice cream.

kay's tart tatin

Felicity and I love the combination of the lemony caramelized apples and crisp, salty pastry of this dessert. When Kay first made it for Felicity, she told me Felicity practically ate the whole pie on her own. I believe her.

Kay says: "The two most important things are the apples and finding the right pan. In England, we prefer to use a Cox's Orange Pippin, but as these are hard to find in North America, a Braeburn should work well in its place. Regarding the pan, I use a 10-inch all-metal sauté pan with sloping sides. No plastic handles, because it needs to go in the oven. Remember: Don't try to take it out without gloves."

---

1. Make the pastry: In a bowl, rub together the flour and butter until you get a lovely fine-bread-crumb texture. Stir in the kosher salt. Add 1 teaspoon of ice water at a time, gently bringing the pastry together until it forms a cohesive dough. Mold it with your hands into a nice smooth ball. Cover in plastic wrap and refrigerate until ready to use.

2. Preheat the oven to 425°F.

3. Make the filling: Place the apples in a bowl with the lemon juice.

4. Spread the butter into the bottom of a 10- to 12-inch ovenproof sauté pan—squish it in with your fingers fairly evenly. Mix the sugar and lemon zest together and sprinkle over the butter.

5. Place the apples, cut-side up, in concentric circles in the prepared pan. If there are any small gaps, just cut the apple pieces to fit. Pour the lemon juice from the bowl over the apples.

6. Place the pan over low heat and melt the butter and sugar slowly. Once it has melted, raise the heat to a gentle bubble and start gently spooning or flicking it over the apples every now and then, making

Serves 4 to 6

FOR THE PASTRY

1⅓ cups all-purpose flour, plus more for dusting work surface

6 tablespoons unsalted butter, cold

1 teaspoon kosher salt

Ice water

FOR THE FILLING

6 to 8 Braeburn apples (about 2 pounds), peeled, cored, and halved

Juice of 1 lemon

3 ounces unsalted butter

3/4 cup superfine sugar

Zest of ½ lemon

FOR SERVING

Whipped cream or crème fraiche

recipe pictured on next page

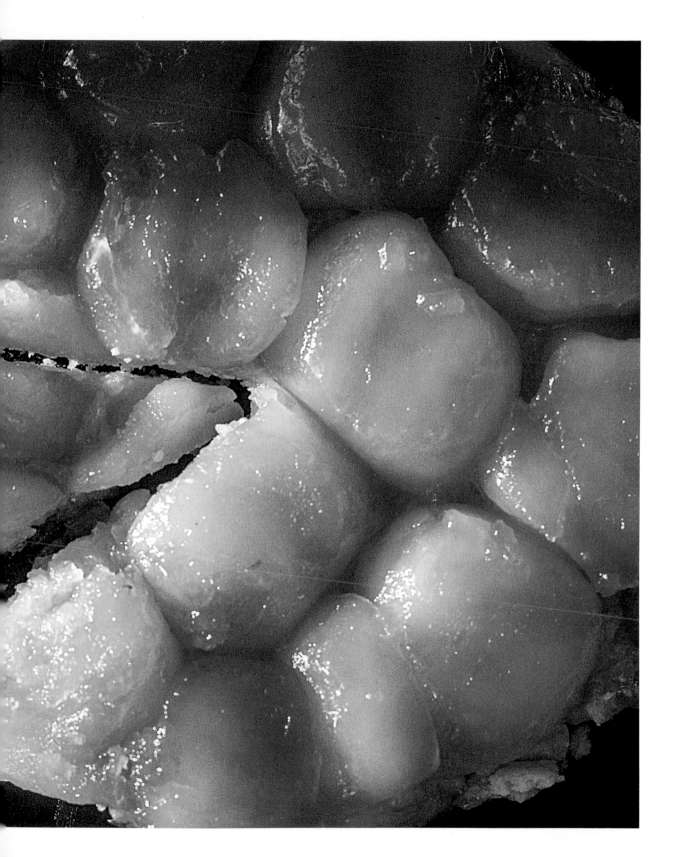

sure to shake the pan to move things around so that nothing sticks or burns, until the whole thing has turned a beautiful shade of sticky amber. This should take 20 to 30 minutes, but keep an eye on it so the caramel doesn't turn too dark. When the caramel is done, remove the pan from the heat.

7. Assemble the dish: Lightly flour your work surface. Take the pastry out of the fridge and roll it out until it's the size you need—10 to 12 inches, depending on your pan. I like to trim a circle out with a knife. Place it over the apple mixture, taking care to tuck the edges down the sides like a little quilt. Prick the surface of the pastry all over (otherwise, the steam will make it soggy) and bake for about 25 minutes, until the pastry is golden and crisp.

8. Remove and let cool for 5 to 10 minutes, then *carefully* turn the tart out onto a platter and serve warm or at room temperature with whipped cream or crème fraîche.

STANLEY'S TIP

A 12-inch Emile Henry pan works very well for this.

blondies

These blondies are delicious, salty, sweet, and chewy. I used to bring Toblerones home for the kids from my travels and they loved them, so we incorporated them into this delectable treat.

———————

1. Preheat the oven to 350°F. Grease and line an 8-inch square baking pan with parchment paper.

2. In a large bowl, sift together the flour and baking powder. Add salt and mix well.

3. In a large saucepan, melt the butter over low heat. Remove the pan from the heat and add the sugar and vanilla. Mix together well. Add the eggs and stir thoroughly to combine. Stir in the flour mixture and the Toblerone pieces. Mix everything together thoroughly.

4. Spoon the mixture into the prepared baking pan. Bake for 25 to 30 minutes, or until cracks start appearing. Don't overcook the blondies, as they will cook a little more as they cool. Let cool completely in the pan before cutting into squares and serving.

Makes about 16

1 cup all purpose flour

2 teaspoons baking powder

Good pinch of kosher salt

6 tablespoons (¾ stick) unsalted butter

1 cup light brown sugar

1 teaspoon pure vanilla extract

2 large eggs, lightly beaten

7 ounces Toblerone, smashed into small pieces

camilla's raspberry ripple lemon cake

Fortunately for us, Camilla loves to bake. She even asked for a mixer for her birthday. Often when she has friends over for the weekend, their Saturday night activity is the creation of something sweet and iced. This is a version of a lemon cake she made for me on my last birthday, although the real present was that she also did the washing up. . . .

———————

1. Make the cake: Preheat the oven to 350°F. Grease an 8 x 4-inch loaf pan with butter and line it with parchment paper.

2. Put all the ingredients except the raspberry jam and the fresh raspberries into a food processor or stand mixer and process until smooth.

3. Divide the batter fairly evenly between two bowls—if anything, put a little less into the bowl that will have raspberries added—and stir the raspberry jam and crushed raspberries into one bowl until it is well mixed. It should be pink and fairly smooth.

4. Pour the batter into the prepared loaf pan one spoonful at a time, alternating the pink and the white batters, like a checkerboard. It will probably take two layers. Take a wooden skewer or knife and make a swirling motion through the cake to make a ripple effect. Tap the loaf pan with a spoon or bang it on the kitchen counter to get rid of any air bubbles.

5. Bake for 45 to 50 minutes, checking the cake after 35 minutes, or until a wooden skewer or a knife tip inserted into the cake comes out clean. Remove from the oven and let cool in the pan for 10 minutes.

6. Meanwhile, make the icing: while the cake is cooling—you want to ice it while it is still a little warm. In a bowl, mix the water and confectioners' sugar together until you have a nice, thick white icing.

Serves 8 to 10

FOR THE CAKE

8 tablespoons (1 stick) unsalted butter, softened

¾ cup superfine sugar

1⅓ cups cake flour

1 tablespoon baking powder

2 large eggs

Finely grated zest of 1 lemon

2 tablespoons good raspberry jam (not too runny)

½ cup fresh raspberries, crushed, plus extra for serving

FOR THE ICING

2 tablespoons water

1 cup confectioners' sugar

6 fresh raspberries (optional)

Fresh raspberries to serve

recipe continued on next page

If you like, place the 6 raspberries in a sieve over your bowl, work them through so the liquid is separated from the seeds, and then mix the pink juice into the icing to give it a beautiful pink hue.

7. Gently turn out the cake onto a wire rack and prick it all over with a fork. This will allow the icing to trickle into the cake. Spoon the icing over the cake, making sure to pick up any drips and pour them over as well. Leave to set.

8. Serve with fresh raspberries on the side.

carrot cake

Felicity says: "This was the cake I used to make with my childhood friend Bea for her to take back to boarding school. It was a way of making her departure a little sweeter and more palatable. It truly is my favorite cake. I like to roast some of the carrots for an extra moist crumb."

―――――――

1. Make the cake: Preheat the oven to 350°F. Grease a 9-inch springform pan with butter and line it with greaseproof paper.

2. Take the three carrots and snap them into rough thirds. Coat them with vegetable oil and stick them in the middle of the oven. Roast for about 45 minutes, until soft. Then remove the carrots from the oven and peel off the skins, leaving the soft flesh inside.

3. Either break up the nuts in a food processor or place them in a plastic bag and break them into pieces with a rolling pin. Place the nuts in a food processor and add the banana and roasted carrots. Process for about 15 seconds until everything is broken up.

4. Add the sugar and eggs. Sift in the flour, salt, baking soda, baking powder, nutmeg, and cinnamon. Add the oil and process everything together for about 15 seconds. Remove the blade from the food processor, scrape down the sides, and mix in the grated carrot by hand.

5. Pour the mixture into the prepared pan. Bake in the center of the oven for 1 hour, until baked through and golden brown on top. A skewer inserted into the center of the cake should come out clean. Turn the cake out onto a wire rack and let cool.

Serves 8 to 10

FOR THE CAKE

3 medium carrots, washed (no need to peel)

Vegetable oil for coating carrots, plus ¾ cup

⅓ cup walnuts, plus several whole for garnish (optional)

⅓ cup blanched almond slivers

1 small to medium banana, ripe

1½ cups soft brown sugar

3 large eggs

2½ cups all-purpose flour

1 teaspoon kosher salt

1 teaspoon baking soda

2 teaspoons baking powder

1 teaspoon freshly grated nutmeg

1 teaspoon ground cinnamon

2½ cups finely grated carrot

recipe continued on next page

FOR THE CREAM CHEESE ICING

4 ounces full-fat cream cheese

1 stick unsalted butter, softened

2 cups confectioners' sugar, sifted

½ teaspoon pure vanilla extract

6. Make the icing: Combine all of the icing ingredients in a food processor and process until well combined and smooth.

7. Take the cooled cake and slice through the middle with a bread knife to create two equal layers. To do this, place the cake on a flat surface with your hand resting on top and then, keeping your knife parallel to the table, gently move through the cake at the halfway point. Ice the tops of both tiers and layer one on top of the other. Leave the cake in a cool place to allow the icing to firm up before assembling.

joanna's chocolate refrigerator cake

Felicity says: "This is a cake full of childhood memories. Mum used to make it for us when we were growing up. It was always very exciting to smell the syrup and chocolate being heated up, or hear the biscuits being bashed. It's so simple to make, and you don't have to be accurate with the measurements. For a start, it's difficult to weigh syrup, and you can pretty much just throw in a whole pack of biscuits and go from there. Mum used to make it with plain digestive biscuits—I prefer to use milk chocolate ones, as they contrast well with the cocoa."

Makes 12 squares

1 pound milk chocolate digestive biscuits

6 ounces golden syrup

16 tablespoons (2 sticks) unsalted butter

2 ounces unsweetened cocoa powder

---

1. Crush the biscuits in large bowl with the end of rolling pin until you have a texture like coarse bread crumbs. In a saucepan, melt the syrup and butter together and whisk in the cocoa. Heat the mixture through—there's no need to boil or simmer, you just want it loose and pourable. Pour the melted ingredients onto the biscuits and mix well. Line a flat dish with parchment paper. Then pour and scrape the mixture into the dish and press flat. Let cool and then refrigerate.

2. Remove the cake from the fridge and let sit at room temperature for a few minutes to make it easier to cut into squares and serve.

STANLEY'S TIP

As a real treat, serve this with Isabel's New York Cheesecake Ice Cream (page 199)—together, they give you a deconstructed cheesecake, pictured opposite.

nanna's scones

Makes 4 very big or 6 normal-size scones

1½ cups all-purpose flour, plus more for dusting

1 tablespoon baking powder

4 tablespoons (½ stick) unsalted butter, cut into small squares

Pinch of kosher salt

1 tablespoon superfine sugar

¾ cup whole milk

Strawberry jam, for serving

Butter, for serving

Whipped or clotted cream, for serving (optional)

Scones are an English teatime institution, served with clotted cream (a regional speciality from the southwest of England), strawberry jam, and butter. Felicity says, "My Nanna served these in a coffee shop she owned when I was growing up. My sister and I loved the privilege of going behind the counter and helping ourselves to these golden, high towers as they came out of the oven."

---

1. Preheat the oven to 400°F. Dust a baking sheet with flour.

2. Sift together the flour and baking powder into a bowl. Then quickly rub the butter into the flour until the mixture resembles fine bread crumbs. Mix in the salt and sugar. Add the milk in stages, mixing it through with a knife. At the last moment, bring the dough together with your hands. Don't overwork the dough.

3. Lightly flour your work surface. Roll out the dough to a thickness of about 1½ inches. If you roll the dough too thin, the scones won't rise the way you want them to.

4. Take a medium or larger biscuit cutter—mine is 3 inches in diameter—and cut as many scones as possible. Then gather up the scraps, reknead, and reroll.

5. Place the scones on the prepared baking sheet and dust the top of each one with some extra flour.

6. For the large scones, bake for 10 to 15 minutes, or until golden and risen. For the medium-sized scones, bake for 8 to 10 minutes.

7. Serve warm with jam and butter or, if desired, clotted or whipped cream.

FELICITY'S TIP

Scones really don't keep very well, so it is best to make them the day you want to eat them.

crêpes

The kids would have me make these for them every morning if they could, but then they would be eating six jars of Nutella a week, as they favor a sweet chocolate filling, so these are only a weekend treat.

————

1. Sift the flour into a bowl with the salt. Then, in a separate large bowl, beat the eggs. Beat the sifted flour into the eggs with a wire whisk, then add the milk ¼ to ½ cup at a time until you have a smooth paste—you don't want any lumps. Beat in 1 tablespoon of the vegetable oil.

2. If you have time, let the batter chill in the refrigerator for 1 hour. However, if the children are hungry, just cook it straight away!

3. In a 8- to 10-inch pan, heat the remaining 1 tablespoon vegetable oil over high heat until the oil has turned translucent and coats the bottom of the pan. Drain off any excess oil. Reduce the heat to medium-low and add a ladleful of the batter to the pan, turning the pan so that you coat its bottom evenly. (A lot of people prefer a nonstick for this, but if you get your pan hot enough, you should be fine.)

4. Once the crêpe's base has turned a light golden color and the batter has solidified, flip the crêpe. It's up to you how adventurous you are here—you can attempt to throw it in the air (a great party trick, but sometimes disastrous!) or you can simply flip it with a spatula.

5. Let the crêpe cook through, and serve. (Nutella seems to be de rigueur in our house, with sliced bananas or strawberries, but sugar and lemon is also popular.) Repeat until you have used up all the batter, or until the kids are full.

Makes 4 to 6, serves 4

1 cup all-purpose flour

Good pinch of fine table salt

2 large eggs

1 to 1¼ cups milk

2 tablespoons vegetable oil

SERVING OPTIONS

Lemon juice

Sugar

Sliced bananas

Nutella

Strawberries

meringues

Makes about 12 meringues

4 egg whites

Pinch of kosher salt

1 cup superfine sugar

We realized that there were a fair few recipes in this book that called for egg yolks—so what to do with the whites? It would be sinful to throw them away! So here is a really simple recipe for light and delicious meringues with a chewy, marshmallow-y center. Have them as they are or sandwich them together with whipped cream or buttercream and some lightly crushed soft fruit.

If you have fewer egg whites than we state here, the basic math works out to be 2 ounces sugar to 1 egg white.

––––––––––

1. Preheat the oven to 250°F. Line a baking sheet with parchment paper.

2. Place the egg whites in a very clean large bowl (make sure it is very clean and dry, or the egg whites won't whisk high enough). Whisk the egg whites with the salt until they form stiff peaks. Beat in 1 tablespoon of the sugar, then beat again until glossy and shiny. Fold in the remaining sugar a few tablespoons at a time, beating well after each addition, until you have a mound of cloud-like meringue.

3. Drop spoonfuls of the mixture onto the prepared baking sheet. Bake for 1 to 1½ hours, until light golden and crisp.

4. Remove from the oven and let cool completely.

isabel's new york cheesecake ice cream

We came up with this one rainy day because Isabel loves New York Cheesecake *and* ice cream. We love to serve it with the Chocolate Refrigerator Cake (page 193), but it is just as delicious on its own, or with some graham crackers crumbled over the top.

You will need an ice cream machine to make this.

***

1. Beat the eggs, sugar, and vanilla in a bowl. In a saucepan, gently heat the cream. Add the cream to the egg mixture and beat well. Pour the mixture back into the saucepan and continue to heat, very gently, stirring all the time until you have a light custard, thick enough to coat the back of a spoon. Do not allow to boil. If it looks like the mixture will split, do not panic! Just pop the pan into a bowl or sink of very cold water and whisk like hell!

2. Remove the pan immediately from the heat and let cool slightly before beating in the cream cheese. Set aside to cool completely, then refrigerate.

3. When you're ready to make the ice cream, remove the custard mixture from the fridge and stir in the sour cream and lemon juice (if using). Churn the mixture in your ice cream machine, following the manufacturer's instructions. Decant the ice cream into an appropriate container and store in the freezer. This ice cream will always be slightly soft (see photo on page 192).

Serves 6 to 8

2 eggs, lightly beaten

1¼ cups superfine sugar

1 teaspoon pure vanilla extract

1½ cups heavy whipping cream

1 8-ounce package Philadelphia cream cheese

¾ cup sour cream

Squeeze of fresh lemon juice (optional)

"spagliato" granita

Serves 6

3½ ounces prosecco

1½ ounces Campari

3½ ounces red vermouth

Juice of 4 oranges

1 tablespoon superfine sugar

Negronis are a favorite cocktail of Felicity's. This light, bright granita with the added lift of prosecco is something we love to serve after a dinner party. *Spagliato* means "spoiled," denoting that it is a Negroni made with prosecco instead of gin.

———

Mix all the ingredients together in a shallow glass dish and put it in the freezer. As it freezes, use a fork to break up the ice crystals that start to form on the edges of the container and move them into the center. Ideally, you want to create a mass of snow-like flakes. It should take 3 to 4 hours in all. Don't forget about it, but don't let it dominate your day—as long as you fork it up every half hour or so, all will be well.

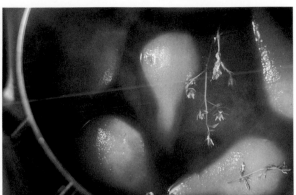

poached pears in red wine

When I was a kid growing up in the sixties and seventies, this, along with Cherries Jubilee, seemed to me the height of sophistication. My mother often made the latter when she threw a dinner party (so does the devilish restaurateur Pascal in *Big Night*), but this is a less volatile treat.

————————

1. Peel the pears, placing them in a bowl with the lemon juice as you go to keep them from discoloring.

2. In a large saucepan, combine the rest of the ingredients and bring to a boil, then reduce the heat to maintain a simmer, making sure the pears are fully submerged in the liquid (weigh them down with the lid of a smaller saucepan, putting a layer of parchment paper between it and the pears, if necessary), and cook for 20 to 30 minutes, until the pears are tender.

3. Remove the pears and put them in the fridge to stop the cooking. Cook the wine over medium heat for 5 to 10 minutes until it has reduced and becomes a light syrup. Strain the syrup to remove the orange peel. Remove from the heat and let cool.

4. Serve the pears with the cooled syrup and some mascarpone cheese.

Serves 6

6 whole pears

Juice of 1 lemon

1 bottle hearty red wine, such as Montepulciano

1 cup superfine sugar

2 to 3 sprigs fresh thyme

Large strip of orange peel

Mascarpone cheese, for serving

strawberries in prosecco

Serves 6

½ pound fresh
strawberries, hulled and
halved or quartered

1 tablespoon
confectioners' sugar
(optional)

1 750 ml bottle very cold
prosecco

This is not so much a recipe but a delicious afterthought and a delightfully alcoholic end to a meal! If strawberries aren't at their best, use peaches or nectarines or even a dash of raspberry puree sweetened with sugar.

———————

If the strawberries are not sweet enough for your liking, toss them gently in the sugar. Divide them equally among six large champagne flutes. Pour the prosecco over the top and serve.

basics

basic stocks

While there are many good quality premade stocks, bouillon cubes, and gelée pots on the market, it's very useful and immensely satisfying to make your own. Here are four that are easy to make and very versatile.

chicken stock

1 raw or cooked chicken carcass

1 carrot, chopped

1 celery stalk, chopped

1 onion, chopped

1 bay leaf

Handful of fresh flat-leaf parsley

10 whole green peppercorns

10 whole black peppercorns

2 large pinches of kosher salt

2½ quarts water

This is probably the stock I make and use the most. If you've recently cooked a chicken but don't have time to make the stock, you can freeze the carcass until you do. Just make sure to thaw it before you begin. The method of bashing the proverbial sh*t out of the carcass is courtesy of our great friend Chef Adam Perry-Lang. This releases all the marrow, thus making your stock extra rich.

———————

1. Cover the chicken bones with parchment and place them in a plastic bag. Then bash the sh*t out of them to release the marrow. The more you bash, the better, but be careful of any chipped bone. Put the bones in a large pot, add the remaining ingredients, and bring the mixture to a boil. Skim off any scum that rises to the surface. Reduce the heat to low and simmer very gently for a couple of hours.

2. Strain the stock through a fine sieve into a large bowl or clean stockpot; discard the solids in the sieve. Store the stock in airtight containers in the fridge or freezer until you need it. It will keep for up to a week in the fridge and up to a month in the freezer.

veal or beef stock

It really isn't that difficult to make your own veal or beef stock, and the difference a great meaty stock makes to stews and ragouts is palpable.

———————

1. Preheat the oven to 400°F.

2. Put the bones in a large roasting dish, toss them with the vegetable oil, and season with a good pinch of salt. Then roast them for about 30 minutes, until the bones are browned and any residual meat has caramelized.

3. Put the bones in a large stockpot, add the remaining ingredients, and bring the mixture to a boil. Skim off any scum that rises to the surface. Reduce the heat to low and simmer very gently for up to 3 hours.

4. Strain the stock through a fine sieve into a bowl or clean stockpot; discard the solids in the sieve. Store the stock in airtight containers in the fridge or freezer until you need it. It will keep for up to a week in the fridge and up to a month in the freezer.

2 pounds veal or beef bones

1 tablespoon vegetable oil

2 large pinches of kosher salt

1 carrot, chopped

1 celery stalk, chopped

1 onion, chopped

Couple of bay leaves

Handful of fresh flat-leaf parsley

Few sprigs fresh thyme

½ tablespoon whole black peppercorns

2½ quarts water

fish stock

2 pounds fish bones and trimmings, including heads

1 onion, chopped

1 carrot, chopped

1 leek, chopped

1 celery stalk, chopped

Handful of fresh flat-leaf parsley

1 bay leaf

A few whole black peppercorns

Place all the ingredients in a large stockpot and add enough water to cover them by about 1 inch. Bring the mixture to a boil. Skim off any scum that rises to the surface. Reduce the heat to low and cook for 20 minutes or so. Strain the stock through a fine sieve into a large bowl or clean stockpot; discard the solids in the sieve. Store the stock in airtight containers in the refrigerator for no more than a couple of days.

quick shrimp stock

1 tablespoon olive oil

1 pound raw shrimp shells

1 bay leaf

A few whole black peppercorns

1 onion, chopped

Handful of fresh flat-leaf parsley

Water, to cover

This one is indispensable when it comes to making Paella (pages 72–73). Peel half the shrimp you need for the paella and use the shells to make this stock.

————

In a large stockpot, heat the olive oil over medium heat. Add the shrimp shells and cook until they turn a reddish-pink. Add the remaining ingredients and enough water to cover them by about 1 inch. Bring the mixture to a boil. Skim off any scum that rises to the surface. Reduce the heat to low and simmer gently for 30 to 40 minutes. Strain the stock through a fine sieve into a large bowl or clean stockpot, pushing the shells against the sieve with the back of a spoon to release as much flavor as possible. This stock doesn't keep, so use it the day you make it.

pasta dough

The "00" or *doppio zero* flour is a reference to the fineness of the flour's grind. Italian millers grade their flour from 00 up to 2—the 2 being closest to whole meal. Ideally for pasta, you want to find a 00 flour ground from durum wheat, which gets its name from the Latin *durum,* meaning hard. It's this quality in the flour that helps the pasta hold its shape and provides it with a silky texture.

————————

1. Mix the flour and salt together and shape it into a small mound. Form a well in the center, crack the eggs into the well, and add the olive oil. Using a fork, start gently incorporating the eggs and the flour, drawing the flour into the center from the top of your well, always trying to maintain the well shape, until you start getting a cohesive pasta dough.

2. Lightly flour a cool work surface and knead the pasta for 6 to 10 minutes until smooth, elastic, and a little sticky. Roll it into a ball and cover in plastic wrap. Set aside to rest at room temperature for 30 to 40 minutes.

3. Roll the pasta through the pasta machine starting on the widest setting, working it gradually thinner until you reach the thinnest setting. Cut the pasta into the desired or required shape for the recipe.

4. If you're making ravioli, you're now ready to assemble them. If you're making lasagna, lay out the sheets on your work surface (or a flour-dusted table) to dry. If you're making a ribbon pasta, pass each sheet through the cutting portion of the pasta machine, then lay the strands out to dry. You can also lay the strands out on baking sheets and freeze them. Once they're stiff, they will keep in airtight containers or frozen for up to a month.

Makes enough for 1 pound pasta or 8 large ravioli

3½ cups all-purpose or "00" flour

1 teaspoon kosher salt

4 large eggs, lightly beaten

1 teaspoon extra virgin olive oil

recipe pictured on next page

pizza dough

Makes two 12-inch pizza bases

1 7-gram packet dry yeast

2 cups warm water

4 cups all-purpose flour, plus more for dusting

1 tablespoon kosher salt

This is my mother's recipe. When we lived in the United States, we made pizza every weekend and swore by it. We always will.

———————

1. First, dissolve the yeast in ½ cup of the warm water. Then, in a large bowl, mix the flour with the salt. Make a well in the center and add the yeasty water. Bring the dough together, adding more of the warm water as you go, until you have a soft dough. You may not need to use all the water—you're looking for the dough to just come together. Lightly flour your work surface and turn out the dough. Knead it into a smooth dough; you may need to add more flour as you go so that it's not too sticky. Form the dough into a ball, put it in a clean bowl, cover loosely, and set aside in a warm place to rise until it has doubled in size, about 2 hours.

2. Divide the risen dough in half. Gently pull and roll out each portion on a floured surface, handling the dough with care and letting it stretch and fall over the backs of your hands until it is a uniform thickness.

3. Top the dough as desired: Spread a thin layer of the Marinara Sauce (page 216) over the dough. Top with sliced mozzarella, a good grating of Parmigiano, and some fresh basil leaves. Put each element on fairly randomly, placing one ingredient where another one isn't. Bake in an oven preheated to 500°F until the pizza's edges are nicely browned—about 15 minutes.

4. You could also top the pizza with Sautéed Mushrooms (page 155), Grilled Spring Onions (page 150), or Roasted Tomatoes (page 170). I love to dot it with Gorgonzola and walnuts, finishing the pizza with a drizzle of honey just when it comes out of the oven.

pesto sauce

Makes 1 cup

1 clove garlic

4 loosely packed cups fresh basil leaves

¾ teaspoon kosher salt

½ cup plus 2 tablespoons extra virgin olive oil

⅓ cup pine nuts

⅓ cup freshly grated Parmigiano-Reggiano

In a food processor, combine the garlic, basil, and salt, and process for about 10 seconds. Remove the lid, scrape down the sides, and process for 10 seconds more. Then, with the motor running, begin to drizzle in ½ cup of the olive oil. Add the pine nuts and cheese and continue to process. Remove the lid and scrape down the sides, then process for 10 seconds more, adding more olive oil until you have the right consistency (it is best to err on the thicker side, so be careful not to add *too* much olive oil). Transfer the pesto to an airtight container, drizzle olive oil over the top to cover it completely, and refrigerate until ready to use. The pesto will keep in the fridge for a week or so. Make sure to top off the pesto with more olive oil after each use.

marinara sauce

Makes approximately 4 cups

3 tablespoons extra virgin olive oil

2 cloves garlic, smashed and halved

½ onion, thinly sliced (optional)

One 35-ounce can whole San Marzano tomatoes

3 fresh basil leaves

Kosher salt

Dried oregano (optional)

Whenever I am on location and move into a new house, the first thing I do is to stock up on all the pantry essentials . . . and the first thing I cook is this sauce. The aroma makes a foreign place feel like home.

———————

In a saucepan, heat the oil over low heat. Add the garlic and onion (if using) and cook to gently soften. Add the tomatoes and crush them in the pan with a fork or potato masher. Add the basil, salt, and oregano (if using). Raise the heat to medium-high and let the tomatoes bubble for 5 minutes. This sweetens them. Reduce the heat to maintain a low simmer and cook for about 30 minutes.

béchamel sauce

Note that béchamel is at its best when it's freshly made. If you have to make it ahead of time, reheat it gently, stirring continuously, until it comes back to the thickness you desire.

---

1. In a small saucepan, heat the milk over low heat until it almost comes to a boil. Don't let it *actually* boil. Remove from the heat and set aside.

2. Meanwhile, in a large, heavy-bottomed saucepan, melt the butter. Add the flour and cook for a couple of minutes, stirring continuously and being sure to not let it take color. You want to remove the floury taste, but not burn the mixture. Remove the pan from the heat and add the milk very gradually, a couple of tablespoons at a time at first, stirring continuously. If you add the milk too fast, you will almost certainly get lumps—if that happens, whisk like hell to break them down. When you've stirred in all the milk, season the sauce with a good pinch of salt and the nutmeg, and place over low heat and stir the sauce until it reaches the thickness you desire.

Makes approximately 2 cups

3 cups whole milk

4 tablespoons (½ stick) butter

¼ cup all-purpose flour

Kosher salt

Good grating of nutmeg

basic mayonnaise

Makes about 1½ cups

1 to 2 cloves garlic, crushed

Kosher salt

2 egg yolks

2 tablespoons extra virgin olive oil

1 to 1¼ cups olive oil

1 to 2 tablespoons lemon juice, to taste

Freshly ground white pepper

This recipe uses white pepper rather than black because no one really wants black flecks in their mayo.

The important things with making mayonnaise are: (1) be not afraid, and (2) you may not have to use all the oil specified—you have to rely on your judgment to know when to stop.

The first time I made mayonnaise was quite amusing to Felicity: "He used seemingly dozens of eggs and pints of olive oil, all to no avail. It was an oily mess. Not a happy camper. Happily, together we have now figured it out."

———————

1. Remove the eggs from the fridge and allow them to come up to room temperature. If your eggs are too cold, your mayonnaise will split.

2. When you're ready to make the mayonnaise, fill a medium bowl with hot water and set it aside to allow the water to warm the bowl. Pour out the water and dry the bowl thoroughly. Grind the garlic and the salt together in the bowl with a pestle. Add the egg yolks and beat them in with a fork. With an electric hand mixer, beat in the extra virgin olive oil. You want to add it very gradually at first, drop by drop, so that the yolks and the oil emulsify. Now, little by little, gradually pour in 1 cup of the olive oil, whisking all the time until the mixture is thick and glossy. Then whisk in the lemon juice. If this makes your mayonnaise too loose, whisk in 2 tablespoons of the remaining olive oil, and maybe the rest of it, until the mayonnaise regains its thick and glossy texture. Finish with some white pepper and some more salt to taste, if you like.

Note: This mayonnaise will keep for no longer than a week.

felicity's cheat's aioli

Felicity says: "When I'm in a hurry I augment store-bought mayonnaise with some roasted garlic (page 20) to give it added depth of flavor. Just squeeze out the flesh of the garlic from 3 cloves onto a chopping board, add a pinch of kosher salt, and, using the side of a knife, mash this to a paste. Add this to approximately 1 cup of mayonnaise and mix through until evenly distributed. You'll have a simple, quick, delicious dip."

acknowledgments

I would like to thank all those who helped bring project to fruition. The wonderful team at Simon and Schuster, particularly the extraordinary Tricia Boczkowski, Jennifer Bergstrom, Louise Burke, Jean Ann Rose, Lisa Litwack, Jaime Putorti, and Paige Cohen, all of whom were so patient, supportive, and generous with their time and talents. Our friend Deborah Schneider for her support. My long time publicist and dear friend, Jennifer Plante, for her devotion and commitment to every project I am involved in. My lovely in-laws, Joanna and Oliver, for their recipes, suggestions, and love of a good meal. My parents, Joan and Stan, for teaching me that food was more than just a thing to sustain you and for encouraging me to be creative in every way possible. Those who have generously shared their recipes with us: Camilla Toniolo, Joan Tucci, Emily Blunt, Tony Shalhoub, Ryan Toal, and Gianni Scappin. Our photographer, Toby Lockerbie, for his brilliant eye, spontaneity, and monklike patience. Fred Hogge, not only for his kindness, generosity, and culinary knowledge but for helping us cook, prep, wash, dry, take notes, type up recipes, and give his expert opinion after tasting every dish! Lottie Birmingham and Andy Galik, our assistants, for running countless times to the green grocer, washing dishes, and organizing our lives. The endlessly energetic and brilliant Kay Plunkette-Hogge for being the best cooking mentor/partner a fellow could have, and for laughing at all of my jokes. To my kids, Nicolo, Isabel, and Camilla, for their joyful and willing participation, their sophisticated palates, their patience with me and the time I spent at the stove with my back to them, whom I love more than anything and whom I am honored to cook for and parent every day. And last but not least to my wife/agent (a frightening combination), Felicity, who made this book happen and whose, intelligence, love, and positive spirit in and out of the kitchen continues to inspire me every day. I would also like to give a hearty thanks to Sub Zero for making the perfect refrigerator for a family our size, or any size, and to Kitchen Aid for their unbeatable appliances.

index